Miss Hel[illegible]

South Side

Address 2902 S. Burr St.

Ft. Wayne

Indiana

Mr. Edward A. Seiffert.

Paul Webb

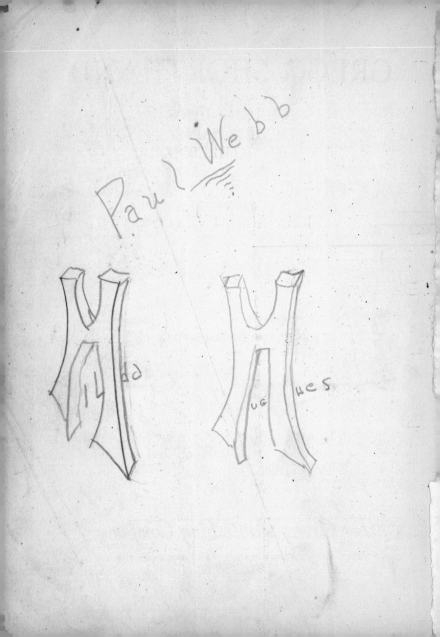

GREGG SHORTHAND

A LIGHT-LINE PHONOGRAPHY *for the* MILLION

By

JOHN ROBERT GREGG

New and Revised Edition

The Gregg Publishing Company

NEW YORK CHICAGO BOSTON SAN FRANCISCO LONDON

A-51-PP-100
Ch

ALLIED PRINTING TRADES UNION LABEL COUNCIL CHICAGO 285

PRINTED IN THE UNITED STATES OF AMERICA

CONTENTS

	PAGE
PREFACE	vii
ABOUT GREGG SHORTHAND	ix
A TALK WITH THE BEGINNER	xiii
THE ALPHABET OF GREGG SHORTHAND	xvi
FIRST LESSON	
Consonants: K, G, R, L, N, M, T, D, H	1
Vowels: The Circles	2
Rules for Joining Circles	3
General Exercise	4
Simple Word-Signs; Phrase-Writing	6
Punctuation, etc.; Reading and Writing Exercises	7
SECOND LESSON	
The Downward Characters: P, B, F, V, Ch, J, Sh	8
Rule for Joining Circles to Oblique Curves	9
Rule for Placing First Consonant	9
General Exercise	10
Word-Signs and Phrases	12
Reading and Writing Exercises	13
THIRD LESSON	
The O-Hook	14
General Exercise	14
Rule for Joining O-Hook	16
General Exercise	16
Word-Signs and Phrases	17
Reading and Writing Exercises	18
FOURTH LESSON	
The OO-Hook	19
General Exercise	19
Rule for Joining OO-Hook	20
Review Exercise on Both Hooks	21
W and Y	21
General Exercise	23

PAGE

Word-Signs and Phrases - 24
Reading and Writing Exercises - 25

FIFTH LESSON
Consonants: S and Th - 26
Rules for Joining S and Th - 26
Z and Th (as in *breathe*) and X Explained - 28
The Combinations Ng and Nk - 29
Simple Prefixes and Suffixes - 29
General Exercise - 30
Word-Signs and Phrases - 32
Reading and Writing Exercises - 33

SIXTH LESSON
Diphthongs: *ū*, *ow*, *oi*, *i* - 34
General Exercise - 34
Vowel Combinations - 36
Word-Signs and Phrases - 37
Reading and Writing Exercises - 38

SEVENTH LESSON
Blended Consonants - 39
Ten, den; tem, dem; ent, end; emt, emd - 39
General Exercise - 40
Def, dev, tive; jent, jend, pent, pend - 41
General Exercise - 41
Men, mem; ted, ded, det; ses; xes - 42
General Exercise - 42
Word-Signs and Phrases - 43
Reading Exercise - 44
Writing Exercise - 45

EIGHTH LESSON
Rules for Expressing R - 46
General Exercise - 47
Rules for the Omission of R - 49
Word-Signs - 50
Reading Exercise - 50
Writing Exercise - 51

NINTH LESSON
Review Exercise on Word-Signs - 52
List of Additional Word-Signs - 54
Reading Exercise - 57
Writing Exercise - 58

TENTH LESSON

PAGE

Compound Words - 59
Derivatives, etc. - 60
General Exercise - 61
The Abbreviating Principle - 62
Exercise on Abbreviating Principle - 64
Days and Months - 66
Figures, etc. - 67
Reading Exercise - 68
Writing Exercise - 69

ELEVENTH LESSON

Phrase-Writing - 70
General Exercise - 71
Word Modifications - 72
Omission of Words - 75
General Exercise - 76
Special Business Phrases - 78
Reading Exercise - 78
Writing Exercise - 79

TWELFTH LESSON

Omission of Vowels - 80
General Principles - 82
Omission of Consonants - 83
General Exercise - 84
Reading and Writing Exercises - 87

THIRTEENTH LESSON

Joined Prefixes - 88
General Exercise - 90
Compound Joined Prefixes - 93
Prefixal Abbreviations - 94
Reading and Writing Exercises - 95

FOURTEENTH LESSON

The "Tr Principle" - 96
General Exercise - 97
Compound Disjoined Prefixes - 99
Derivatives of Words Ending in "ct" - 100
Reading Exercise - 100
Writing Exercise - 101

FIFTEENTH LESSON PAGE
Disjoined Prefixes - - - - - - - - - - - 102
General Exercise - - - - - - - - - - - - - 104
Compound Disjoined Prefixes - - - - - - - 106
Reading Exercise - - - - - - - - - - - - 107
Writing Exercise - - - - - - - - - - - - 108
SIXTEENTH LESSON
Joined Suffixes - - - - - - - - - - - - - 109
General Exercise - - - - - - - - - - - - 111
Compound Joined Suffixes - - - - - - - - - 114
Reading Exercise - - - - - - - - - - - - 115
Writing Exercise - - - - - - - - - - - - 116
SEVENTEENTH LESSON
Disjoined Suffixes - - - - - - - - - - - - 117
General Exercise - - - - - - - - - - - - 119
Reading Exercise - - - - - - - - - - - - 121
Writing Exercise - - - - - - - - - - - - 122
EIGHTEENTH LESSON
Disjoined Suffixes—continued - - - - - - - 123
General Exercise - - - - - - - - - - - - 126
Reading Exercise - - - - - - - - - - - - 128
Writing Exercise - - - - - - - - - - - - 129
NINETEENTH LESSON
Advanced Phrase-Writing - - - - - - - - 130
Omission of Words - - - - - - - - - - - - 130
Intersection - - - - - - - - - - - - - - 131
Indication of "ing" - - - - - - - - - - - 132
Modification of Word Forms - - - - - - - 133
Reading Exercise - - - - - - - - - - - - 137
Writing Exercise - - - - - - - - - - - - 138
TWENTIETH LESSON
Initials - - - - - - - - - - - - - - - - 139
States and Territories - - - - - - - - - 140
Principal Cities - - - - - - - - - - - - 141
Points of the Compass, etc - - - - - - - - 143
General Rules - - - - - - - - - - - - - 144
Reading Exercise - - - - - - - - - - - - 147
Writing Exercise - - - - - - - - - - - - 148
SUPPLEMENTARY
A Short Vocabulary - - - - - - - - - - - 149
Shorthand as a Means of Mental Culture - - - - 153

PREFACE

In the Preface to the first edition of this system, I said:

> The endeavor of the author has been to compile a system so simple as to be readily acquired by the humblest capacity and those possessed of little leisure, and yet rapid enough to reproduce verbatim the fastest oratory. In presenting his work to the public he asks for nothing beyond an impartial investigation, and with perfect confidence awaits the result.

The subsequent history of the system has justified the confidence expressed at that time. Gregg Shorthand has demonstrated its superiority to the older systems in simplicity, legibility and speed—and there are to-day nearly a million writers of the system. In beginning the preparation of this edition it was my intention to make some radical changes in the manner of presenting the principles; but in proceeding with the revision I was forced to the conclusion that it would be a mistake to depart materially from the general plan and form of the previous edition. No better evidence of the popularity and success of the previous edition could be given than the fact that, although nearly a million copies of it have been sold, there has been very little demand for revision except requests for the inclusion of those changes and improvements that have been made in the course of the past few years.

This edition, then, retains the general plan and form of the previous edition, but much of the material contained in it is arranged in more logical sequence, and the illustrations are chosen with greater care, with a view to developing quickness in the application of its rules and principles. An attempt has been made to state some of the rules more clearly than was done in the old book, and to put them into language better adapted to the comprehension of young students.

In the system itself few changes have been found necessary or desirable. Some new word-signs and extensions of advanced principles have been introduced, but all of these are in harmony with the fundamental principles of the system. All of them have been subjected to very careful trial in practical work before they have been adopted.

In sending forth this book I desire to express my heartfelt appreciation of the suggestions that have come to me from writers, from reporters and from teachers who are using the system in all parts of the world. These suggestions have been of great service to me in the preparation of this presentation of the system.

JOHN ROBERT GREGG.

NEW YORK, June 17, 1916.

About Gregg Shorthand

History.—Gregg Shorthand was first published in 1888, in two little paper-covered pamphlets, under the title, "Light-Line Phonography." Five years later a revised and greatly improved edition was published under the title, "Gregg Shorthand." It was not until 1897, however, that the author was able to publish the system in *book* form.

There are few more interesting or inspiring stories of success than the career of Gregg Shorthand in the years that have elapsed since its publication in book form. To-day Gregg Shorthand is the standard shorthand system of America. It is taught in more than seven thousand five hundred schools—that is to say, in more than eighty-five per cent of the schools that teach shorthand. It has been adopted in the public schools of 3900 cities and towns, and has superseded the older systems in a large number of these cities by formal action of Boards of Education.

Wins World's Championship.—In the 1921 contest of the National Shorthand Reporters' Association, Mr. Albert Schneider, a writer of Gregg Shorthand, won the world's championship, defeating the largest number of writers to participate in one of these contests among them three former champions. In the championship tests, consisting of dictations for five minutes each at 200 words a minute literary matter, 240 words a minute jury charge, and 280 words a minute testimony, he made an average percentage of 97.94. Only one other contestant qualified. Mr. Schneider also transcribed the literary matter dictations at 215 and 175 words a minute and established new world records on both of these, tying with Mr. Willard B. Bottome, an official reporter of the Supreme Court of New York City, on the 175 with three errors. In the 215 dictation *he made the highest net speed ever attained in any contest at any speed on matter of this kind*—211.2 words a minute. The extraordinary legibility of Mr. Schneider's notes was shown by the fact that he transcribed five of the highest speed dictations in the time allotted for the three championship dictations. Mr.

Schneider was but twenty years old at the time of the contest, and was the youngest and least experienced writer to win the championship.

Other Public Triumphs.—In 1910 a writer of Gregg Shorthand, Mr. Fred H. Gurtler, won the final contest for the famous Miner Medal, in the Fifth International Shorthand Speed Contest held under the auspices of the Eastern Commercial Teachers' Association. Gregg writers won *first*, *second* and *third* places. All of the Gregg writers qualified—ten of the fourteen writers of other systems failed.

In the 1911 shorthand speed contest of the National Shorthand Reporters' Association, a writer of Gregg Shorthand, Mr. Charles L. Swem (then eighteen years of age), established a world's record for *accuracy* on literary matter at 170 words a minute for five minutes, and with a net speed of 237 words a minute exceeded the previous world's record by ten words a minute on a judge's charge to a jury dictated at 240 words a minute.

In the 1912 speed contest of the National Shorthand Reporters Association, Mr. Swem achieved a net speed of 268 words a minute for five minutes on testimony, and defeated three of the former champions as well as eighteen other contestants—all of them experienced reporters.*

In 1912, in the shorthand contest held at the Business Exhibition, London, a writer of Gregg Shorthand, Mr. Ernest W. Crockett, of Liverpool, won the Junior Shorthand Championship, having *less than one per cent errors in his transcript.*

Awarded Medal of Honor at Panama-Pacific Exposition.—At the Panama-Pacific International Exposition, in 1915, Gregg Shorthand was awarded the Medal of Honor, the highest award ever granted a system of shorthand by any Exposition and the only award ever granted which was based on the results accomplished by students in a model school conducted under the observation of

*Mr. Swem was Personal Secretary and Official Reporter to President Wilson for eight years. He was twenty years of age when he received the appointment at the White House.

the International Jury of Awards. The Gregg system was selected by the Exposition Authorities for use in the model school of business in the Palace of Education—a school designed to demonstrate the most advanced methods in business education.

Principles of the System.—Needless to say, Gregg Shorthand is a radical departure from the old lines of shorthand construction, for it is only by a radical departure that such marked superiority in results can be accomplished.

The following synopsis will enable the reader to understand the leading features of the system:

(1) No Compulsory Thickening.—May be written either light or heavy.

(2) Written on the Slope of Longhand, thus securing a uniform manual movement.

(3) Position Writing Abolished.—May be written on unruled paper, and in one straight line.

(4) Vowels and Consonants Are Joined, and follow each other in their natural order.

(5) Angles Are Rare.—Curves predominate.

[(1)–(5): As in ordinary writing]

This brief synopsis will suffice to show that the aim of the author has been to adhere to those natural principles which govern ordinary writing. By a practical combination of these elements as a foundation, the system secures to the writer, *with very little practice*, that perfect command of the characters which is productive of the best results, and is only obtained by years of persistent, painstaking practice if the old geometric systems are employed.

TO SUM UP:

Easy to Learn.—Gregg Shorthand may be learned in from one-third to one-half the time required by the old systems. The records made by its writers prove this beyond all question.

Easy to Read.—Gregg Shorthand is the most legible shorthand in existence. In the public shorthand speed contests, writers of the system have established the *highest official world's records for accuracy* of transcripts on solid, difficult matter. These records were made in competition with experienced reporters who used the older systems, and in contests conducted by reporters and teachers who wrote such systems. (Full particulars of these contests will be sent by the publishers on application.) Manifestly, the insertion of the vowels, the absence of shading, the elimination of position-writing and the elimination of the minute distinctions of form necessary in the old systems, all contribute to legibility.

Easy to Write.—The easy, natural appearance of the writing in Gregg Shorthand appeals to every impartial investigator. The absence of distinctions between light and heavy characters, the continuous run of the writing along one line, as in longhand, instead of constant changes of position—now *on* the line, then *above* the line, and then, perhaps, *through* or *below* the line—will be noticed at a first glance. Next, the investigator will probably attribute much of the natural, pleasing appearance of the writing to that uniform slant of the writing, with which both hand and eye are familiar. Only those who have had previous experience with shorthand, however, will be able to appreciate fully how much elimination of numerous dots and dashes—minute marks that have to be placed with great precision alongside the strokes—contributes to easy, continuous, effortless writing.

Superior in Speed Possibilities.—Writers of Gregg Shorthand have demonstrated in public speed contests, under the most trying conditions, that the system has greater speed possibilities than any other system. A boy of nineteen (who began the study of Gregg Shorthand in a night school less than four years previously) established a record of 268 words a minute net for five minutes, defeating three former champions and eighteen other experienced and capable reporters. The contest committee consisted of seven shorthand reporters, all of whom were writers of other systems. When a mere boy can do this, after such a brief experience, there can be no question that this system of shorthand possesses greater speed possibilities than any of the older systems.

A TALK WITH THE BEGINNER

Success in any study depends largely upon the *interest* taken in that particular subject by the student. This being the case, we earnestly hope that you will realize at the very outset that shorthand can be made an intensely fascinating study. Cultivate a love for it. Think of it as the highest form of writing, which is itself the greatest invention of man. Be proud that you can record the language in graceful lines and curves. Aim constantly to acquire artistic skill in executing those lines and curves. You *can*, if you *will*, make the study of shorthand a perfect joy instead of a task. Its possession has been coveted by the wisest of men and women, for it is not only a practical instrument in commercial work, but a much prized and valuable accomplishment and a means of mental culture.

Be Thorough.—Skill in anything is attained by repetition; therefore do not shirk the careful, painstaking practice on the elementary forms given in the Manual. Write each outline many times, and aim always at the attainment of ease and exactness in execution.

Your future success depends to a very large extent on the way you do your work now. In order that your progress may be sure and rapid, master each lesson before you proceed with the next.

At first, write slowly and carefully; aim at accuracy rather than speed, but do not *draw* the characters. You must understand at the outset that shorthand must be *written;* but you must also impress upon your mind that whatever you write you must read, hence the necessity for good penmanship. As skill in executing the movements is obtained, the speed may be increased until the forms are written rapidly. Some attention should be given to acquiring a capacity for writing *individual* outlines rapidly without hesitation, and with a free movement of the hand.

Aim to acquire a smooth style of writing; execute each character with an easy, *continuous* motion of the pen, and pass directly to the next without unnecessary movements. A halting, jerky movement is fatal to speed, and may be almost always traced to indecision, caused by unfamiliarity with the forms. At first carefully analyze the words. To do this it is, of course, necessary for you to think of them in detail; but after you have determined the correct outline, practice it and think of it as a *whole.*

Facility in the use of shorthand depends largely upon the stock of outlines you have at your ready command. Note the use of that word *ready.* This means that you should master all the forms given in the Manual by writing them many times. This will not only impress the forms on your mind so that you will not have any hesitation in recalling them, but will give you facility in writing them. In shorthand it is not sufficient to *know* how to write a word—you must not only know the form but be able to write it quickly. Hence the necessity for much *repetition practice* in writing the forms.

If, in addition to the words given in the Manual, you can add to your stock of outlines other words written under the same principles you will have gained a great deal—will have laid a broader foundation for advanced work which will lessen the time required to attain efficiency.

Devote Much Time to Reading Well-Written Shorthand.—By doing this you will become not only a fluent reader, but you will enlarge your writing vocabulary. Unconsciously you will imitate in your own work the easy execution of the forms shown in the printed plates. All expert writers have devoted much time to reading shorthand.

In addition to the work outlined in this Manual, we strongly recommend the use of the exercises given each month in the Learners' Department of the *Gregg Writer.* These exercises can be used with great advantage from the very first lesson. Each number contains many helpful suggestions, and a number of shorthand pages that afford valuable exercises in reading and writing for students at all stages of advancement.

Don't Get Discouraged.—The complete mastery of shorthand and typewriting is worthy of your best efforts, and if you devote yourself earnestly to that work there can be no such thing as failure.

THE UNITED STATES OF AMERICA
PANAMA-PACIFIC INTERNATIONAL EXPOSITION
SAN FRANCISCO, MCMXV.
EDUCATION
AGRICULTURE
MINING
ARTS & SCIENCES
MANUFACTURES
TRANSPORTATION
CELEBRATING THE OPENING OF THE PANAMA CANAL
THE INTERNATIONAL JURY OF AWARDS HAS CONFERRED A
MEDAL OF HONOR
upon
THE GREGG PUBLISHING COMPANY
for a Collective Exhibit showing Efficiency of GREGG SHORTHAND, RATIONAL TYPEWRITING
OFFICE TRAINING FOR STENOGRAPHERS, by means of a Class of Students being trained
in the Use of These Methods, also for Bound Volumes of the Gregg Writer.
PANAMA

The Alphabet of Gregg Shorthand

CONSONANTS

Written forward:

K G R L N M T D TH

Written downward:

P B F V CH J S SH

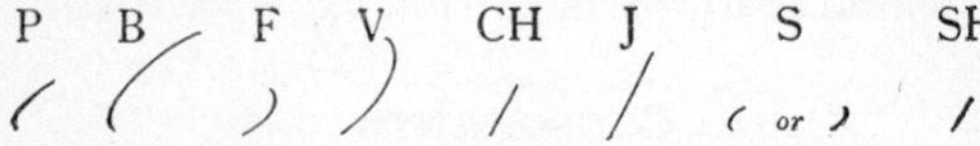

H NG NK

(A dot)

VOWELS

A-group

Short	ă	as in	*cat*
Medium	ä	" "	*calm*
Long	ā	" "	*came*

O-group

Short	ŏ	as in	*hot*
Medium	*aw*	" "	*audit*
Long	ō	" "	*ode*

E-group

Short	ĭ	as in	*din*
Medium	ĕ	" "	*den*
Long	ē	" "	*dean*

OO-group

Short	ŭ	as in	*tuck*
Medium	o͝o	" "	*took*
Long	o͞o	" "	*doom*

DIPHTHONGS

	Composed of		
ū	*ē-o͞o*	as in	*unit*
ow	*ä-o͞o*	" "	*owl*
oi	*aw-ē*	as in	*oil*
ī	*ä-ē*	" "	*isle*

FIRST LESSON

1. Shorthand is written by *sound;* thus *aim* is written *ām* (long sound of *a*), *cat* is written *kăt*, *knee* is written *nē*.

CONSONANTS

2. The alphabet should be mastered in sections, as given in these lessons. It will be noticed that the consonants are arranged in pairs, according to their affinity of sound, and are distinguished by a difference in length. There is no absolute standard as to length, as the characters, being founded on ordinary writing, vary in size, slant, etc., according to the personal habits of the writer. The size of the characters given in this manual will be a safe standard to adopt. The characters for the consonants in this lesson are derived from an elliptical figure, thus:

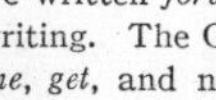

K G R L N M T D H

NOTE: All these characters are written *forward* from left to right, and T, D struck *upwards* from the line of writing. The G given in this lesson is called *gay*, being the hard sound as in *game*, *get*, and not the soft sound heard in *gem*, *magic*. The aspirate H is indicated by a dot placed over the vowel. The student should practice all these characters until he can write them without the slightest hesitation.

VOWELS

3. In writing by sound there are twelve distinct vowels, which are arranged in four groups, and three closely related sounds are placed in each group. In this lesson we have the first two groups, which for convenience are named the "A" group and the "E" group.

4. The *short* sound of *a*, as heard in *cat*, *ran*, is expressed by the large circle; the *medium* sound, as heard in *calm*, *ark*, is expressed by the large circle with a dot beneath the circle; the *long* sound, as heard in *ate*, *may*, is expressed by the large circle with a dash beneath the circle.

ă		*as in*	mat	m ă t	
ä		*as in*	calm	k ä m	
ā		*as in*	gate	g ā t	

5. The *short* sound of *i*, as heard in *din*, *rid* (not the long sound of *i*, heard in *dine*, *ride*), is expressed by the small circle; the sound of *e*, as heard in *get*, *net*, is expressed by the small circle with a dot beneath the circle; the *long* sound of *e*, as heard in *me*, *eat*, is expressed by the small circle with a dash beneath the circle.

ĭ		*as in*	knit	n ĭ t	
ĕ		*as in*	net	n ĕ t	
ē		*as in*	neat	n ē t	

NOTE: The dot and dash are useful to indicate the exact vowel sounds in unfamiliar or in isolated words, but otherwise they are seldom used.

RULES FOR JOINING CIRCLES

6. The circle is written on the *inside of curves*, and on the *outside of angles*.

Inside Curves

eke	ē k		era	ē r a	
key	k ē		rat	r ă t	
ale	ā l		take	t ā k	

Outside Angles

team	t ē m		rail	r ā l	
meet	m ē t	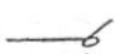	gain	g ā n	

at beginning of straight Providing the circle engages the within

7. Before or after straight lines, or between two straight lines running in the same direction, the circle is written forward—as the hands of a clock move.

	Before			*After*	
aim	ā m		me	m ē	
hat	h ă t		day	d ā	

Between

mean	m ē n		deed	d ē d	

8. Between two reverse curves the circle is turned on the back of the first curve.

kill	k ĭ l		gear	g ē r	
wreck	r ĕ k		lake	l ā k	

Between a horizontal curve and a straight line the circle is written within the curve.
Examples:

METHOD OF PRACTICE

9. The following list of words should now be copied. In doing this, particular attention must be paid to the *sounds* of each word. If the student will repeat the sounds as he writes the word, it will help to impress the forms upon his memory and at the same time familiarize him with the process of note-taking.

GENERAL EXERCISE

knee	n ē		tact	t ă k t	
keen	k ē n		tray	t r ā	
kick	k ĭ k		train	t r ā n	
ache	ā k		treat	t r ē t	
acre	ā k r		nail	n ā l	
acme	a k m ē		tale	t ā l	
neck	n ĕ k		lay	l ā	
cake	k ā k		deem	d ē m	
ark	ä r k		rim	r ĭ m	
eat	ē t		reed	r ē d	
kit	k ĭ t		arid	a r ĭ d	
hit	h ĭ t		rainy	r ā n ĭ	
had	h ă d		hack	h ă k	

eddy	ĕ d ĭ	ill	ĭ l
writ	r ĭ t	hill	h ĭ l
came	k ā m	mill	m ĭ l
creed	k r ē d	attic	ă t ĭ k
cream	k r ē m	tickle	t ĭ k l
merry	m ĕ r ĭ	ticket	t ĭ k ĕ t
lane	l ā n	trick	t r ĭ k
lamb	l ă m	deck	d ĕ k
lady	l ā d ĭ	deacon	d ē k n
rack	r ă k	decay	d ē k ā
ready	r ĕ d ĭ	reel	r ē l
maim	m ā m	gray	g r ā
grim	g r ĭ m	eagle	ē g l
rally	r ă l ĭ	arena	a r ē n a
get	g ĕ t	narrate	n ă r ā t
rig	r ĭ g	marine	m a r ē n
linen	l ĭ n ĕ n	hatred	h ā t r ĕ d
drama	d r ä m a	camera	k ă m ĕ r a
rag	r ă g	tyranny	t ĭ r a n ĭ
lick	l ĭ k	etiquette	ĕ t ĭ k ĕ t

There are two humps joinings ... and "gay-r". All other curves join with a "glide".

Simple Word-Signs

10. A large proportion of all written and spoken language is made up of a few simple words. For such words brief forms called word-signs are provided. Those given here should be memorized immediately:

can		in, not		he	
go, good		am, more		I	
are, our		at, it		a, an (dot)	·
well, will		would		the (th)	
					up

Phrase-Writing

11. The joining of simple words is a great help to speed in writing shorthand, but it is a difficult art to acquire if its acquirement be deferred until the habit has been formed of writing common words separately. The student should, therefore, practice it diligently from the very beginning of his study. For such practice the simple phrases here given will serve as models:

in the		I would		it will not	
I can		I am		I can not	
I will		at the		in our	
would not		it will		can the	

PUNCTUATION, ETC.

12. The *period* is expressed by ⁀, the end of a *paragraph* by >, the *dash* by =, the *hyphen* by ⫽ (two short dashes struck upward), and the *interrogation* by ×. Capitals and proper names may be indicated by two short dashes under the outline. The parentheses may be expressed by the ordinary marks with short dashes through them ( ). Other punctuation marks are written in the usual way.

READING EXERCISE

WRITING EXERCISE

1. Ellen Terry read the drama well.
2. Helen Keller can read in-the dark.
3. The rain will make the day dreary.
4. The enemy may make an attack in-the rear.
5. The League team will meet at-the Arena.

SECOND LESSON

THE DOWNWARD CHARACTERS

13. The characters for the consonants in this lesson are derived from another elliptical figure; thus 

P	B	F	V	CH	J	SH

NOTES: All these characters are written downwards. CH is pronounced *chay,* not *see-aitch;* and SH is called *ish,* not *es-aitch.* SH is a mere tick.

The following memory aids will be helpful:

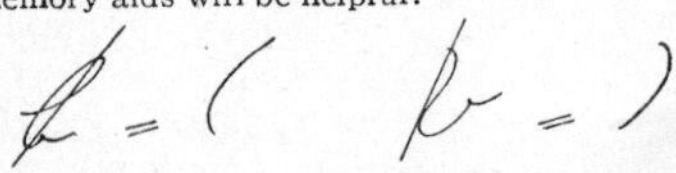

14. In the writing of F, V, a rather vertical inclination is desirable in order that the curve may join easily with other characters. In forming the combinations *fr, fl,* it is not necessary to make an angle. The motion is just the same as in writing a part of Y in longhand; thus

fig	f ĭ g	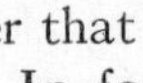	free	f r ē	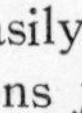
vain	v ā n	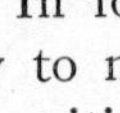	frame	f r ā m	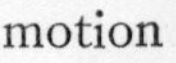
fail	f ā l	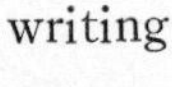	flash	f l ă sh	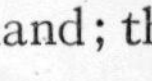

15. The circle may assume the form of a loop where more convenient.

dash	d ă sh	cheat	ch ē t
fame	f ā m	lap	l ă p

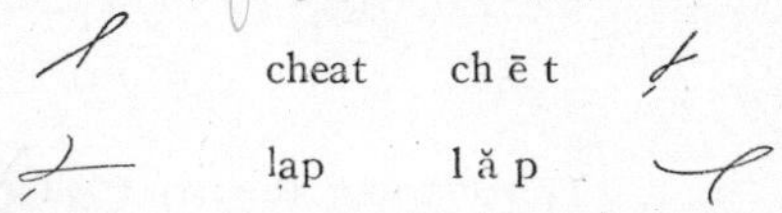

16. Between an oblique curve—such as P, B, F, V—and a straight line, the circle is placed on the outside.

palm	p ä m	Dave	d ā v
beat	b ē t	knave	n ā v

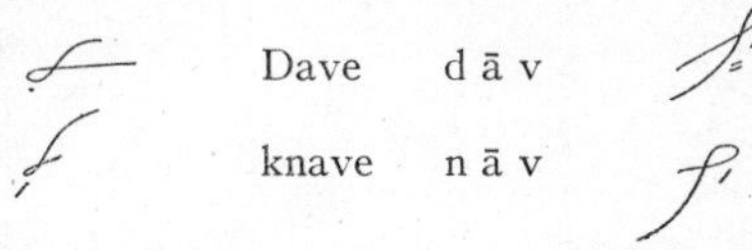

17. The base of the first consonant of a word rests on the line of writing.

map	m ă p	fetch	f ĕ ch
cave	k ā v	chief	ch ē f

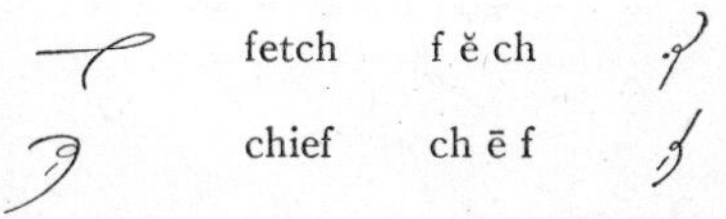

18. The following words illustrate the application of the rules for joining circles to the consonants given in this lesson:

Inside Curves (Par. 6).

Outside Angles (Par. 6).

Joined to Straight Lines (Par. 7).

Between Reverse Curves (Par. 8).

Between Oblique Curves and Straight Lines (Par. 16).

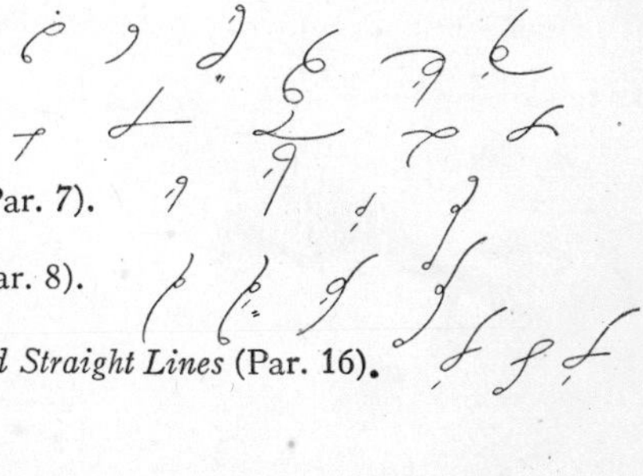

General Exercise

edge	ĕ j	jig	j ĭ g
able	ā b l	apple	ă p l
fear	f ē r	peal	p ē l
beer	b ē r	appeal	ă p ē l
fish	f ĭ sh	cheap	ch ē p
feed	f ē d	chap	ch ă p
play	p l ā	beak	b ē k
cheek	ch ē k	back	b ă k
reap	r ē p	beam	b ē m
peep	p ē p	balm	b ä m
Jap	j ă p	chain	ch ā n
nap	n ă p	catch	k ă ch
cab	k ă b	shake	sh ā k
peach	p ē ch	shame	sh ā m
preach	p r ē ch	bread	b r ĕ d
tab	t ă b	bridge	b r ĭ j
gem	j ĕ m	shave	sh ā v
pale	p ā l	fray	f r ā
sherry	sh ĕ r ĭ	feel	f ē l

ledge	l ĕ j	Arab	ă r a b
allege	ă l ĕ j	chill	ch ĭ l
pledge	p l ĕ j	Jack	j ă k
nib	n ĭ b	rage	r ā j
brief	b r ē f	page	p ā j
chin	ch ĭ n	vague	v ā g
calf	k ä f	dip	d ĭ p
rave	r ā v	rich	r ĭ ch
grave	g r ā v	navy	n ā v ĭ
shade	sh ā d	cliff	k l ĭ f
half	h ä f	shaggy	sh ă g ĭ
badge	b ă j	vim	v ĭ m
brain	b r ā n	abate	a b ā t
valid	v ă l ĭ d	heavy	h ĕ v ĭ
trap	t r ă p	Java	j ä v a
crash	k r ă sh	parish	p ă r ĭ sh
trash	t r ă sh	palate	p ă l a t
beef	b ē f	flinch	f l ĭ n ch
brave	b r ā v	beetle	b ē t l
hitch	h ĭ ch	avail	ă v ā l

WORD-SIGNS AND PHRASES

put	let, letter
be, but, by	little
been, bound	market, Mr.
before, behalf	reply
belief, believe	represent
for	teach
form, from	check
have	for the
change, which	I have
shall, ship	I have not
about	in which
after	I shall
ever-y	I shall not
any	I shall have
name	from the
give-n	would be
gave	in reply
please	please ship

NOTE: The rule given in Par. 17 applies to phrases.

Reading Exercise

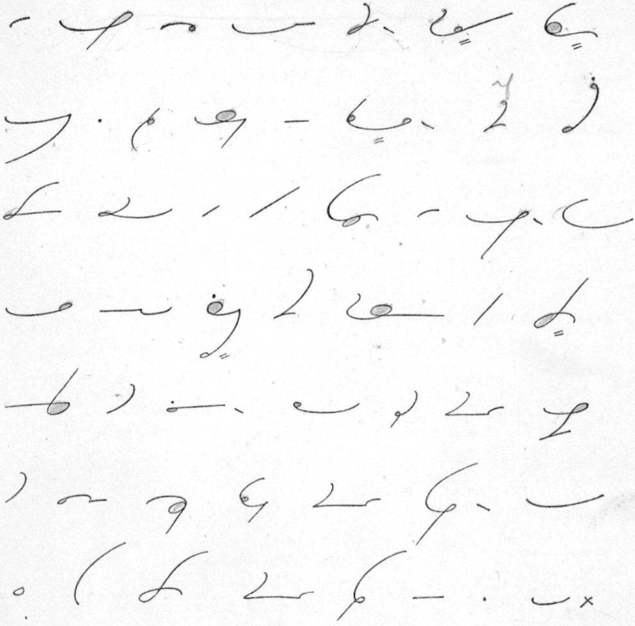

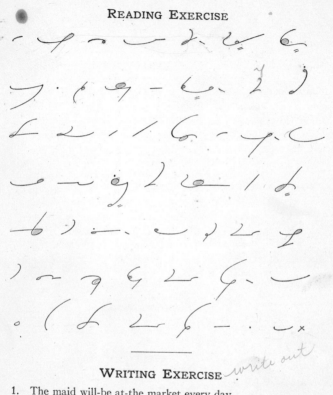

Writing Exercise

1. The maid will-be at-the market every day.
2. Phoebe Cary will teach her French.
3. The team will-be ready for-the match game.
4. Henry came back from-the navy after he had achieved fame.
5. The range in-the kitchen will bake good bread.
6. Jennie will-have the meal ready in about an hour.
7. Please pay for-the ticket in cash for I-can-not take a check.

THIRD LESSON

The O-Hook

19. The lower part of the elliptical figure (called the *o-hook*) represents the short sound of *o*, as heard in *hot, top;* the hook with a dot beneath it expresses the sound of *aw*, as in *awe, law*; the hook with a short dash beneath it expresses the long sound of *o*, as in *owe, no.*

ŏ	*as in*	rot	r ŏ t
aw	*as in*	raw	r aw
ō	*as in*	wrote	r ō t

General Exercise

hot	h ŏ t	Shaw	sh aw
ought	aw t	shawl	sh aw l
taught	t aw t	show	sh ō
odd	ŏ d	shoal	sh ō l
nod	n ŏ d	toad	t ō d
Maud	m aw d	foe	f ō
mode	m ō d	foam	f ō m

loaf	l ō f	paw	p aw
cope	k ō p	pawn	p aw n
coach	k ō ch	jaw	j aw
rod	r ŏ d	dodge	d ŏ j
blow	b l ō	lodge	l ŏ j
botch	b ŏ ch	talk	t aw k
hobby	h ŏ b ĭ	broad	b r aw d
fraud	f r aw d	dough	d ō
wrought	r aw t	Jove	j ō v
dot	d ŏ t	obey	ō b ā
ball	b aw l	hope	h ō p
hog	h ŏ g	fop	f ŏ p
blot	b l ŏ t	chop	ch ŏ p
rogue	r ō g	Paul	p aw l
pillow	p ĭ l ō	pole	p ō l
shallow	sh ă l ō	beau	b ō
elbow	ĕ l b ō	arrow	ă r ō
rope	r ō p	John	j ŏ n
polo	p ō l ō	bone	b ō n
bore	b ō r	motto	m ŏ t ō

20. The O-hook is placed on its side *before* N, M, R, L, except when preceded by a downward character, as in *bore*, *bone*, *pole*, *foam*, *John*.

on	ŏ n	hall	h aw l
or	aw r	dome	d ō m
moan	m ō n	Nome	n ō m

General Exercise

nor	n aw r	home	h ō m
orb	aw r b	flown	f l ō n
own	ō n	knoll	n ō l
whole	h ō l	drawn	d r aw n
hollow	h ŏ l ō	blown	b l ō n
aroma	a r ō m a	tone	t ō n
core	k ō r	atone	a t ō n
known	n ō n	door	d ō r
roam	r ō m	adore	a d ō r
roll	r ō l	loan	l ō n
comb	k ō m	alone	a l ō n
coal	k ō l	mole	m ō l
omit	ō m ĭ t	dawn	d aw n

goal	g ō l	holy	h ō l ĭ
tall	t aw l	Nora	n ō r a
brawny	b r aw n ĭ	Cora	k ō r a

WORD-SIGNS AND PHRASES

all	told
beyond	very
body	of the
call	of all
care	of which
company, keep	of our
fall, follow	in favor
far, favor	in our favor
friend-ly	on the
glad	on our
judge	on which
most	on which the
of	in regard
public, publish	I told
real, regard	on behalf

Reading Exercise

Writing Exercise

1. The team will haul the heavy load of coal.
2. Judge Lodge would-not keep the letter from-the public.
3. He will-pay for-the lot if Mr. Cone will take a check drawn in-our-favor.
4. I-can-not very well follow the form given in-the letter.
5. After the ball game Laura came home in-the launch.
6. The good ship Jane dashed on a rock, but all the people reached the shore.

FOURTH LESSON

The O͞O-Hook

21. The upper part of the small elliptical figure (called the *oo-hook*) represents the short sound of *u*, heard in *hum*, *dumb* (not the long *u* heard in *use*, which will be given later); the hook with a dot beneath it expresses the sound of *oo*, as in *took*, *foot*; the hook with a short dash beneath it expresses the long *oo*, as in *doom*, *boom*.

ŭ	*as in*	tuck	t ŭ k
o͝o	*as in*	took	t o͝o k
o͞o	*as in*	tomb	t o͞o m

General Exercise

hut	h ŭ t	doom	d o͞o m
tug	t ŭ g	shove	sh ŭ v
shut	sh ŭ t	hug	h ŭ g
shoot	sh o͞o t	rut	r ŭ t
to	t o͝o	shoe	sh o͞o
do	d o͞o	shook	sh o͝o k

foot	f ŏŏ t	up	ŭ p
cuff	k ŭ f	dug	d ŭ g
hush	h ŭ sh	jug	j ŭ g
gush	g ŭ sh	fudge	f ŭ j
honey	h ŭ n ĭ	huff	h ŭ f
duck	d ŭ k	pool	p ōō l
hood	h ŏŏ d	fool	f ōō l
hook	h ŏŏ k	toot	t ōō t
dove	d ŭ v	oven	ŭ v n
puff	p ŭ f	tough	t ŭ f
who	h ōō	ruddy	r ŭ d ĭ
whom	h ōō m	chuckle	ch ŭ k l
huddle	h ŭ d l	boom	b ōō m
tattoo	t ă t ōō	lucky	l ŭ k ĭ

22. The OO-hook is always placed on its side *after* N or M; it is also placed on its side *after* K or G *when followed by* R or L. ("always")

nun	n ŭ n	mug	m ŭ g
mud	m ŭ d	mood	m ōō d
muff	m ŭ f	cool	k ōō l
moon	m ōō n	gull	g ŭ l

Review Exercise on Both Hooks

hot	h ŏ t		loam	l ō m	
hut	h ŭ t		loom	l o͞o m	
home	h ō m	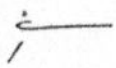	rot	r ŏ t	
hum	h ŭ m		rut	r ŭ t	
moan	m ō n		bone	b ō n	
moon	m o͞o n		boon	b o͞o n	
mode	m ō d		coach	k ō ch	
mood	m o͞o d	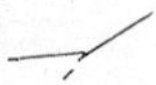	gush	g ŭ sh	
dome	d ō m		coal	k ō l	
doom	d o͞o m		cull	k ŭ l	

W and Y

23. When followed by a vowel, W has the sound of *o͞o*, as o͞o-ā-t—*wait*. W is therefore expressed by the oo-hook.

we	w ē		wall	w aw l	
weave	w ē v		woe	w ō	
wait	w ā t		wool	w o͝o l	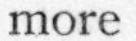

24. In the body of a word it is generally more convenient to express *w* by a horizontal dash under the vowel, but this dash may often be omitted.

twig	t w ĭ g	equity	ĕ k w ĭ t ĭ
twin	t w ĭ n	dwell	d w ĕ l
quick	k w ĭ k	headway	h ĕ d w ā

25. In words beginning with *a-h* or *a-w*, followed by a vowel, *a* is expressed by a dot placed on the line close to the next character.

ahead	a h ĕ d	awake	a w ā k
away	a w ā	ahem	a h ĕ m

26. Wh is pronounced *hw*, as h-w-ē-l — *wheel*, hence the dot for *h* should be written first.

whit	hw ĭ t	whack	hw ă k
whig	hw ĭ g	whim	hw ĭ m

27. Y is equivalent to ē, as ē-ō-r — *yore*, and is therefore represented by the small circle.

yacht	y ŏ t	yore	y ō r
yawn	y aw n	yawl	y aw l

NOTE: When the combination *yo* or *yaw* precedes R or L, the hook is not placed on its side. this is done to prevent the hook from becoming obscured in rapid writing

28. At the beginning of a word *yĭ* or *ye* is expressed by a small loop, and *ya* by a large loop. When necessary to denote the exact shade of vowel sound, the dot or dash is placed beneath the loop.

ye	yē		yet	yĕ t	
yea	yā		yellow	yĕ l ō	
year	yē r		Yale	yā l	

General Exercise

way	w ā		acquit	ă k w ĭ t	
wave	w ā v		quail	k w ā l	
wade	w ā d		Broadway	b r aw d w ā	
wake	w ā k		roadway	r ō d w ā	
wage	w ā j		await	a w ā t	
weed	w ē d		awoke	a w ō k	
widow	w ĭ d ō		wheel	hw ē l	
weep	w ē p		wheat	hw ē t	
walk	w aw k		whip	hw ĭ p	
wash	w ŏ sh		whiff	hw ĭ f	
watch	w ŏ ch		yam	yă m	
wove	w ō v		Yarrow	yă r ō	
quack	k w ă k		yoke	y ō k	

Word-Signs and Phrases

above	of your
become, book	to you
could	do you
full-y	you have
great	you have not
look	we have
move	we have not
much	you can not
should	we can not
sure-ly	we will
upon	from you
work	your letter
world	if you have
yes	if you will
you, your	if you can

W is omitted in the following words:

week	when
were	what
where	won-one

Reading Exercise

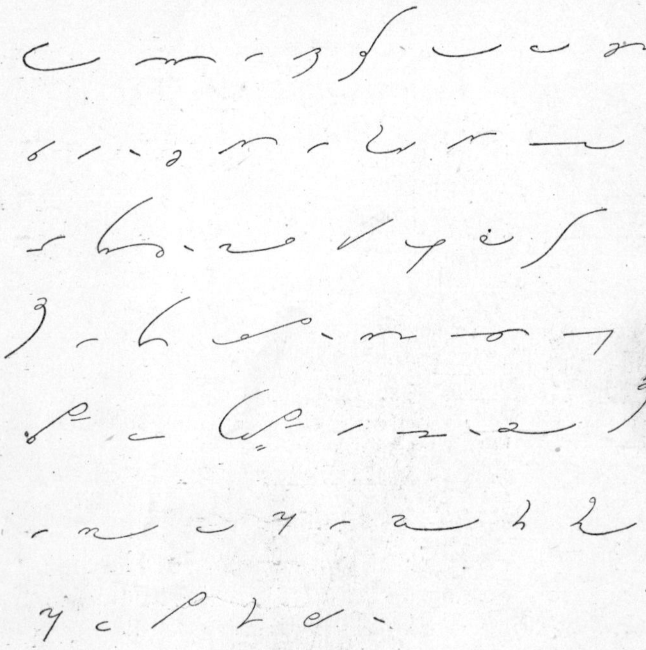

Writing Exercise

1. The wheel of-the wagon caught in a rut of-the rough road.
2. The pony ran away but the groom caught him.
3. Edwin should-have told you about-the affair before the letter reached you.
4. You-may do the work in your own way if-you-are sure you-can do it well.
5. The mud in-the road will-reach up to-the hub of-the wagon wheel.

forward ith
backward sth

FIFTH LESSON

S AND TH

29. From the small elliptical figure given in the last lesson two small curves are obtained which are written downwards to express the very common letter S, and upwards to express Th.

S	TH
or	or
down	*up*

NOTE: It is very important to keep steadily in mind that the curves for S are written *downwards*, while those for TH are written *upwards* and at a greater inclination. The following is a useful memory aid:

RULES FOR JOINING S AND TH

30. When S is joined to a curve, the S is written in the same direction as the curve to which it is joined, thus securing a *uniform movement.* A circle vowel occurring at the joining does not affect the application of this rule.

spray	safe	makes
reaps	face	case
pass	skate	slay
sphere	sick	sales

NOTE: When S precedes a down stroke, the base of the *down stroke* rests on the line.

When S begins an outline the next consonant goes on the line.

31. When S is joined to T, D, N, M, the S is used which forms a sharp angle. A circle vowel occurring at the joining does not affect the application of this rule.

stay	odds	smack
set	days	same
nets	snow	leans
said	seen	knees

32. When S is joined to Sh, Ch, J, the S is used which is written with the clockwise movement—called the "comma S."

sash	sage	chess

33. In words consisting of S or Th, or both, and a *circle* vowel, S or Th should be written with the clockwise movement.

Circle and S	*Circle and Th*	*Combinations*
as	heath	these
see	hath	sees
essay	thee	Seth

34. The clockwise Th is given the preference, but when joined to O, R, L, the other form is used.

thick	though	moth
theme	throw	earth
doth	athlete	health

35. In words beginning with *so*, the "comma S" is used.

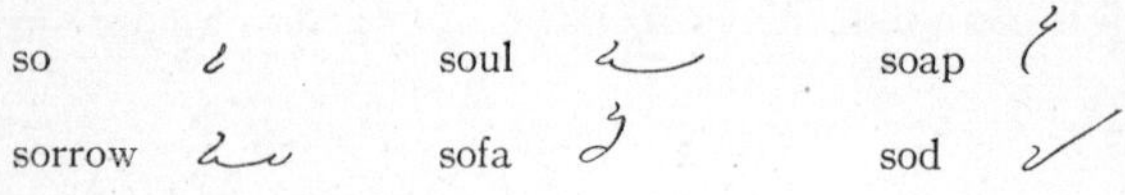

36. The combination *us* is written without an angle at the beginning of words, or when it follows a down stroke or K, G.

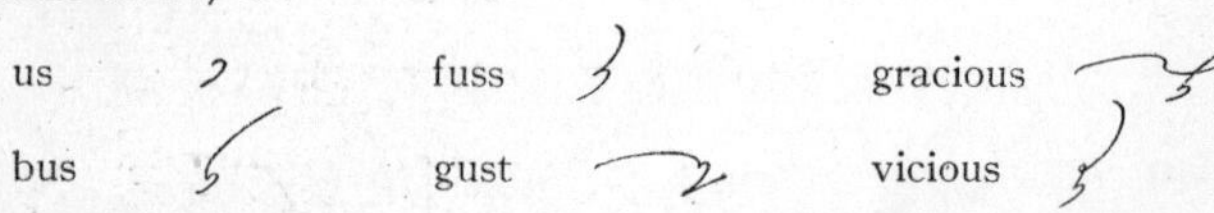

37. Z is represented by the sign for S, but an oblique dash marks the distinction in isolated words. If necessary, the Th heard in *breathe* may be distinguished from the sound heard in *breath* in the same manner.

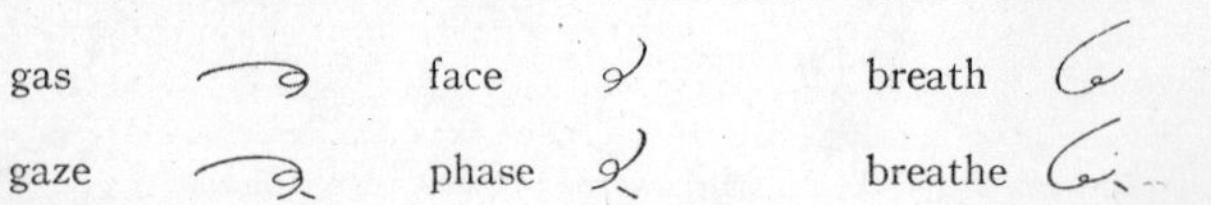

NOTE: The sound of *zh*, heard in *azure, rouge, garage,* may be distinguished from *sh* by the oblique dash, but this is necessary only where it is desired to mark the precise sounds of foreign words.

38. The letter X may be expressed at the end, or in the body of words, (but not at the beginning), by a slight modification of the curve for S, as shown in the following examples:

39. The sound of Ng, heard in *long*, is expressed by N written in a slightly downward direction; and Nk (which is sounded *ngk*, as *rang-k—rank*) by a longer sign.

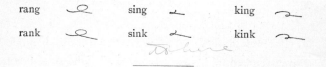

rang	sing	king
rank	sink	kink

SIMPLE PREFIXES AND SUFFIXES

40. The prefixes *con*, *com*, *coun* are expressed by K, and the vowel is omitted in the prefixes *en*, *in*, *un*, *em*, *im* when the prefix is followed by a *consonant*. The prefix *ex* is expressed by *es*.

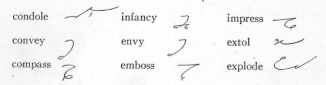

condole	infancy	impress
convey	envy	extol
compass	emboss	explode

41. The suffix *ing* or *thing* is expressed by a dot placed beneath or close to the preceding letter; *ings* is expressed by S in the same place, the S being written contrary to the hands-of-a-clock movement.

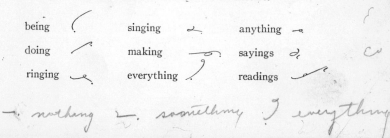

being	singing	anything
doing	making	sayings
ringing	everything	readings

42. The suffix *ly* is expressed by the small circle, and *ily, ally* by a loop.

only	calmly	prettily
early	readily	totally

43. The suffix *tion, sion* (*shun*) is expressed by SH.

nation	session	action
oration	motion	fashion

General Exercise

say	guess	link
seem	chase	throat
save	sleepy	both
sap	serene	booth
solemn	steel	gang
scratch	stray	thief
scream	city	death
scrip	snake	swear
score	smash	switch
hymns	smith	sweet
miss	fasten	swim

NOTE: When *sw* is followed by T, D, N, or M, the *w* is expressed by the hook.

trace	salad	loath
terrace	threat	thud
shoes	throne	preface
shows	myth	spring
husky	wrong	*con*done
dusky	acid	*com*plex
hustle	bath	*con*cave
audacious	wing	*com*bat
zealous	zero	*coun*ty
efface	siege	*en*rich
ethics	thus	*in*famous
hasty	suffix	*un*fit
sabre	elixir	rela*tion*
saucy	applause	*ex*pres*sion*
essays	stab	*in*va*sion*
Jessie	sedate	shipp*ing*
sprain	theft	feel*ings*
elapse	sashes	thick*ly*
story	sober	brut*ally*
sparrow	plank	craft*ily*

Word-Signs and Phrases

ask	than, then
business	that
cause, because	their, there
course	them
desire	they
else, list	thing, think
inclose	this
instan-$^{t}_{ce}$	those
is, his	was
long	is the
must	is this
next	is there
other	there is
receive	this is
some	in these
soon	for that
speak, speech	he was
state	there was
such	in such

READING EXERCISE

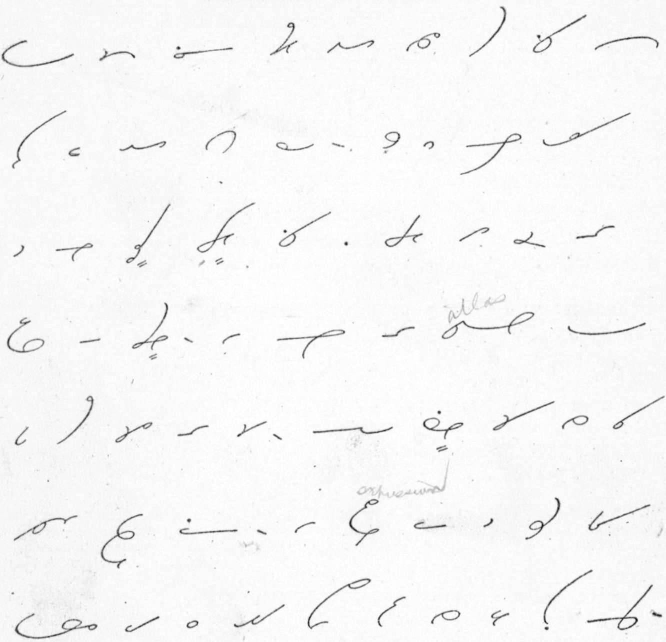

WRITING EXERCISE

1. The book of essays by John Burroughs was-given a long notice in-the papers.
2. I-think that such a motion was made early in-the session.
3. I-shall-not wait for a letter from Mr. King as-the book is on-the press.
4. We-inclose a list of things which we-shall need very soon.
5. The speech by Nicholas Murray Butler was on-the ethics of teaching.

SIXTH LESSON

DIPHTHONGS

44. A pure diphthong is the union in one syllable of two simple vowels uttered in rapid succession. The diphthongs are therefore expressed by joining the circles and hooks representing the vowels of which they are composed.

ū		*as in*	fume	f ū m	
ow		*as in*	now	n ow	
oi		*as in*	oil	oi l	
ī		*as in*	die	d ī	

NOTE: The diphthong ū is a combination of ē and o͞o; *ow*, of ä and o͞o; *oi*, of *aw* and ē. The sign for the diphthong ī is a large circle with an indentation—resembling a combination of ä and ē, which, if uttered in rapid succession, yield a sound almost equivalent to ī. This sign for ī is generally called "the broken circle."

GENERAL EXERCISE

hue	h ū		fine	f ī n	
feud	f ū d		huge	h ū j	
cow	k ow		mute	m ū t	
toy	t oi	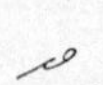	bough	b ow	
annoy	a n oi		Hoyle	h oi l	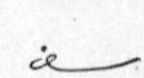
sky	s k ī		try	t r ī	

unique	ū n ē k	thy	th ī
ounce	ow n s	humid	h ū m ĭ d
toil	t oi l	sigh	s ī
ripe	r ī p	scout	s k ow t
youth	ū th	Nile	n ī l
thou	th ow	vow	v ow
mine	m ī n	price	p r ī s
Roy	r oi	rhyme	r ī m
cue	k ū	apply	ă p l ī
guide	g ī d	tile	t ī l
alloy	ă l oi	comply	*com* p l ī
chime	ch ī m	invite	*in* v ī t
adjoin	a j oi n	enjoy	*en* j oi
fight	f ī t	impugn	*im* p ū n
mouth	m ow th	exude	*ex* ū d
noise	n oi s	mightily	m ī t *ily*

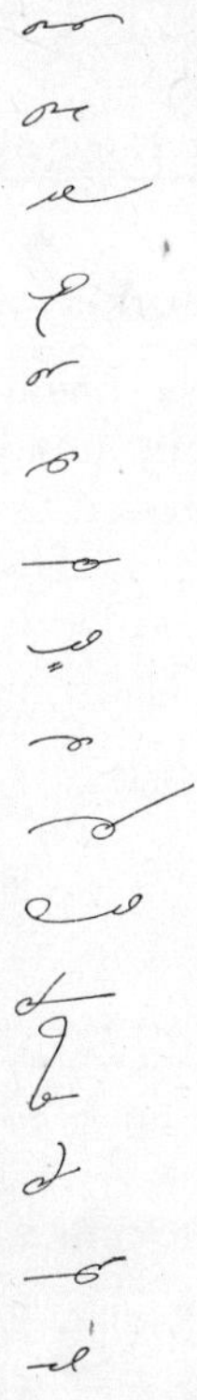

NOTES: (a) The rules governing the joining of the circles apply to the diphthong ī. In the words *Nile*, *tile*, for instance, the sign is placed outside the angle, as is done in *nail*, *tale*.

(b) In some words it will be found unnecessary to write the line through the large circle to express the diphthong. For example, it is sufficient to write *mat* for *might*, as "it mat (might) be," and *ma* for *my*, as "in ma (my) opinion," etc. Other common examples are: *life*, *quite*, *lively*.

word signs - quite
life lively

VOWEL COMBINATIONS

45. Consecutive vowels which do not form a pure diphthong are joined in their natural order.

Leo	l ē ō	olio	ō l ĭ ō
Owen	ō ĕ n	cameo	k ă m ĕ ō
Noah	n ō a	snowy	s n ō ĭ

NOTE: When long ō is followed by a small circle, as in *Owen*, (ō ĕ n), the dash is usually placed beneath the hook.

46. Any vowel following the diphthong *i* is expressed by the small circle within the large circle.

via	v ī a	lion	l ī ŭ n
fiat	f ī ă t	science	s ī ĕ n s
dial	d ī a l	iota	ī ō t a

NOTE: When *io* begins a word it is written (as in *iota*, given above) with the same movement as *o* in longhand, which it resembles in appearance.

47. Where necessary, short *i* followed by *a* as in *mania*, is expressed by the large circle with a *dot* placed within it; and *e* followed by any large circle vowel sound by the large circle with a *dash* within it. These distinctions are seldom necessary.

mania	m ā n ĭ a	Olympia	o l ĭ m p ĭ a
medial	m ē d ĭ a l	ammonia	ă m ō n ĭ a
create	k r ē ā t	Lydia	l ĭ d ĭ a

○ = ī + any vowel
⊙ = ĭ + any sound of a.
⊖ = ē + " " "

48. There are a few words in which there are no consonants. In such words the dot for the aspirate, or the marks distinguishing the vowel sounds, should be used.

ah!	who	ye
awe	hue, hew	yea
owe, oh!	hay	woe
hoe	high	woo

Word-Signs and Phrases

allow	point, appoint	I find
behind	right, write	wire
find	side	please wire
how, out	use	please write
kind	usual-ly, wish	write me
light	while	your kind letter
like	why	on this side
new	wife	I would like

Special Business Phrases

Dear Sir	Yours truly	Yours very truly
Dear Madam	Very truly yours	Yours respectfully

Reading Exercise

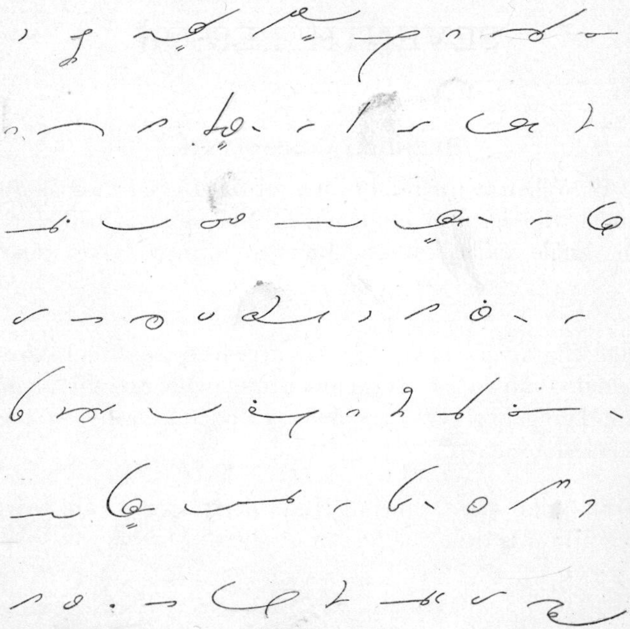

Writing Exercise

1. Julia Marlowe will-not play Ophelia this year.

2. If-you-find that Mr. Boyd is out of-the city, please-wire-me so that I-can get other help for you.

3. Please-write-me fully as-to what you do about increasing the price on-the lots in Butte.

4. Before we publish the book we-must find out about the size of type which you-wish us to use.

5. The chimes will ring in the new year.

SEVENTH LESSON

BLENDED CONSONANTS

49. When two straight lines form an obtuse or blunt angle, the natural tendency of the hand is to "slur" the angle and allow the lines to form a curve, thus:

The characters have been so arranged that many frequent combinations form an obtuse angle, and this angle not being observed, the lines blend naturally in the form of a curve.

50. All of the following blended consonants are written upwards from the line of writing:

TEN, DEN	*as in*	tenor	denote
TEM, DEM	*as in*	temper	demolish
ENT, END	*as in*	paint	bond
EMT, EMD	*as in*	prompt	deemed

NOTES: (a) As the combinations are pronounced as syllables, minor vowels occurring between the consonants are omitted, but diphthongs and strongly accented vowels are inserted. For instance, *dean, dine, team, tame, dome, dime,* are written in full. The blend is used, however, in words ending in *tain* as *detain.*

(b) Although the blends *ent, end, emt, emd* are pronounced as syllables, just as *sh* is pronounced *ish,* the vowel preceding the blend is seldom omitted, except at the beginning of a word, as in *entry, entail.*

General Exercise

tenets	detain	temple
tenant	threaten	attempt
tenacious (a)	tendency	demur
dense	attendance	wisdom
*con*dense	timid	entry
*con*densa*tion*	freedom	entail
*con*tinent	kingdom	plenty
*con*demn	*con*templa-*tion*	moaned
*in*ten*tion* (b)	anatomy	dawned
*ex*ten*sion*	phantom	fastened
*con*ten*tion*	autumn	lamed
sweeten	sanctum	seemed
latent (b)	brand	steamed
mutiny	lined	exempt
stencil	signed	shamed
mutton	faint	Indian
obtain	gained	addenda (b)

Notes: (a) The rule given in Paragraph 16 applies to the circle between the blended consonants and straight lines as in the word *tenacious*.

(b) Where it is possible to use either *ten, den,* or *ent, end,* the *ten, den* blend is given the preference.

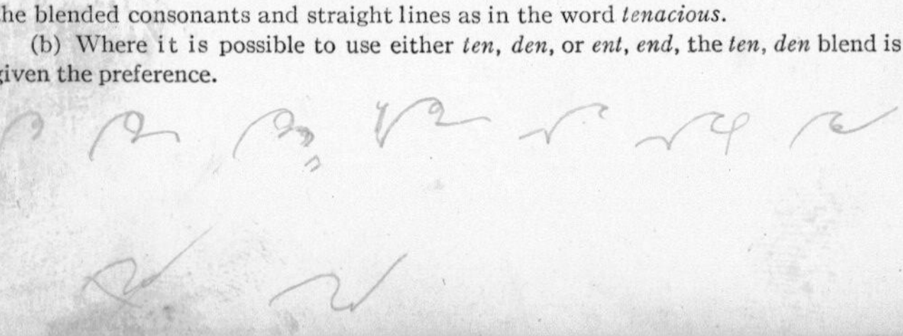

51. In joining *d* to *f* or *v*, and *j* to *ent*, *end*, the angle is obscured in rapid writing, and the combination is written with one impulse of the pen.

DEF-V, TIVE *as in* defeat native

JENT-D, PENT-D *as in* gentle happened

NOTE: It will be found that *tive* generally occurs at the end of words, as in *native*, and cannot be confused with *def*, *dev*, which generally occur at the beginning of words, as in *defame*.

GENERAL EXERCISE

defy	deficit	genteel
edify	restive	Gentile
edifice	festive	legend
deface	motive	regent
defame	attentive	*con*tingent
defense	tentative	tangent
devout	cheapened	pageant
divine	ripened	depend
divide	rampant	spent
diffidence	opened	*ex*pend
devise	cogent	*im*pend*ing*

52. The syllables *men*, *mem* are expressed by lengthening *m*, that is, by joining *m* and *n; ted*, *ded*, *det*, by a long stroke upwards, equal to *t* and *d* joined; *ses* or *sus*, by joining the two signs for *s; xes*, by joining *x* and *s*.

MEN, MEM	*as in*	men*tion*	memory
TED, DED, DET	*as in*	heated	seated
SES	*as in*	passes	faces
XES	*as in*	boxes	mixes

NOTES: The combination *det* usually occurs at the beginning of words, as in *detach*, *detest*, while *ded*, *ted*, usually occur at the end of words.

The stroke is used to express *ted*, *ded* after short words only, a disjoined dash being more convenient in most words as explained in Par. 53.

GENERAL EXERCISE

man	effeminate	Roman
many	nominate	romance
menace	examine	Ottoman
minute	maintain	famine
month	minimum	human
amen	stamina	Manhattan
acumen	women	common*ly*
immense	omen	detach
emanate	ominous	detec*tion*
memoir	remain	waited

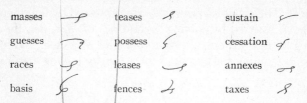

masses	teases	sustain
guesses	possess	cessation
races	leases	annexes
basis	fences	taxes

NOTE: In rapid writing the first *s* in *ses* may become obscure, and yet the second *s*, being written contrary to the rule for writing a single *s*, clearly indicates the plural form. Compare *face, faces, case, cases, pass, passes.*

53. At the end of many words *ted*, *ded*, and sometimes *ed*, may be expressed by *t* placed beneath or close to the preceding character.

invited	divided	demanded	printed

54. Advantage may be taken of the blending principle in phrase writing, thus: *t-me* for *to me*, *t-do* for *to do.*

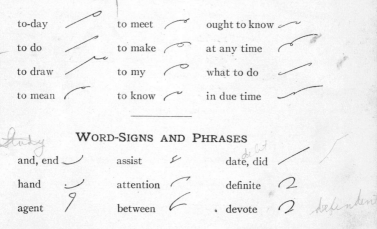

to-day	to meet	ought to know
to do	to make	at any time
to draw	to my	what to do
to mean	to know	in due time

WORD-SIGNS AND PHRASES

and, end	assist	date, did
hand	attention	definite
agent	between	devote

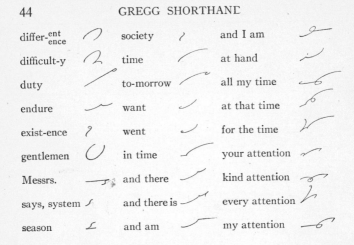

differ-ent/ence	society	and I am
difficult-y	time	at hand
duty	to-morrow	all my time
endure	want	at that time
exist-ence	went	for the time
gentlemen	in time	your attention
Messrs.	and there	kind attention
says, system	and there is	every attention
season	and am	my attention

READING EXERCISE

Review 1st 7 lessons Friday

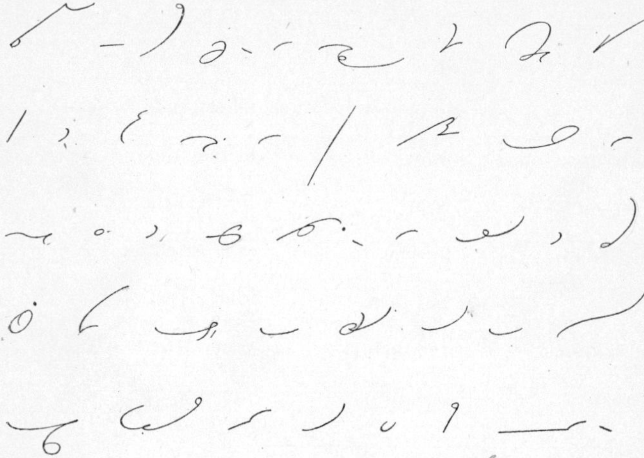

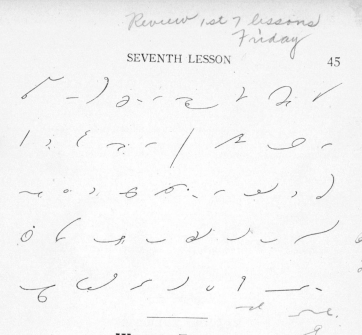

WRITING EXERCISE

1. The society asks for different working conditions and a minimum wage law.

2. The memoirs of-this famous man read like a romance; such a book will-be an inspiration to-me.

3. Andrew Temple will study printing and book binding in the evening classes at the Manhattan Academy.

4. Your-letter reached me, but I-have had no time to-make the definite reply demanded.

5. That you-are in business means that you-are doing something for-which mankind is willing to-give you money.

6. We-can-not grant the extension of-time you-wish, and if-the money does-not reach us by-the date mentioned, we-shall draw on-you through our bank.

7. The auditor who was sent to examine the books for-the season had to devote a month to-the work.

Monday

EIGHTH LESSON

RULES FOR EXPRESSING R

55. The circle or loop is written with a reverse movement to express R:

(a) Before or after straight lines, or between two straight lines in the same direction.

Before		*After*		*Between*	
art		tar		tart	
arm		mar		marmot	
harsh		share		tardy	

(b) Between a horizontal and an upward character.

mart	cart	lard	garden

(c) Between a downward character and T, D, N, M.

pert	barn	chart	farm

NOTE: As there is a tendency in rapid writing to curve a straight line when it is followed by a circle, the distinctive method of joining the circle when reversed after Ch, J, illustrated in *chart* (compare with *pert*), is adopted to prevent any possibility of misreading.

pertain period

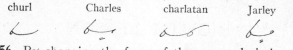

(d) Between SH, CH, J, and L.

churl   Charles   charlatan   Jarley

56. By changing the form of the reversed circle to a *loop* at the end of a straight line, the letter S is added.

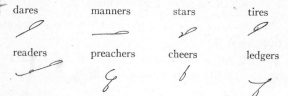

dares   manners   stars   tires

readers   preachers   cheers   ledgers

57. Before straight lines S in *ser*, *cer*, *sar*, and Th in *ther*, *thir*, may be written contrary to the usual method of joining to express R.

sermon   assert   serge   sardine

concern   concert   exert   insert

desert   third   thirty   Thermos

General Exercise

heart   army   harness

hearty   hard   Armenia

heartily   harm   earn

yearn
yard
Yarmouth
harmony
Armada
arch
hermit
hurt*
urge*
near
mere
jeer
dear
domineer
anger
tire
attire
dart
mutter

oyster
barter
dirty
Tartar
tender
cashier
mermaid
murmur
murder
martyr
marten
girder
alert
billiard
Hilliard
poniard
card
carter
cartridge

guarantee
courtesy
Hibbard
pardon
bird
burden
spared
shepherd
shirt
charter
journey
sojourn
adjourn
germ
Charlotte
hammers
farmers
soldiers
surname

*It is generally more facile to use the circle for the obscure vowel sound heard in *ur*.

58. The letter R is omitted without reversing:

(a) In many words containing *ar, er:*

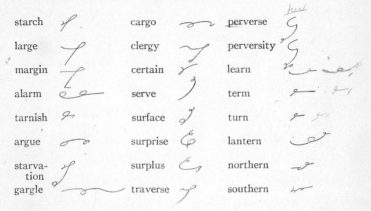

starch	cargo	perverse
large	clergy	perversity
margin	certain	learn
alarm	serve	term
tarnish	surface	turn
argue	surprise	lantern
starvation	surplus	northern
gargle	traverse	southern

(b) In many words containing *or*:

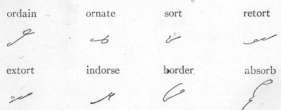

ordain	ornate	sort	retort
extort	indorse	border	absorb

(c) In words beginning with *war, wor*:

war	warn	ward	worse

59. The reversing principle is used to express L in the following words:

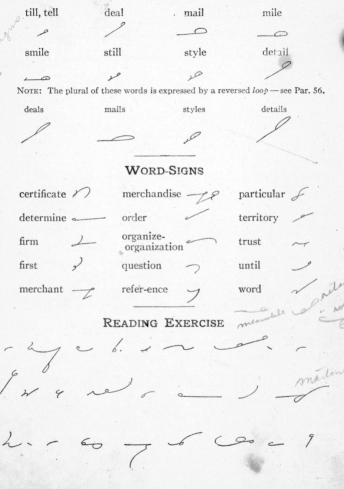

till, tell	deal	mail	mile

smile	still	style	detail

NOTE: The plural of these words is expressed by a reversed *loop* — see Par. 56.

deals	mails	styles	details

WORD-SIGNS

certificate	merchandise	particular
determine	order	territory
firm	organize-organization	trust
first	question	until
merchant	refer-ence	word

READING EXERCISE

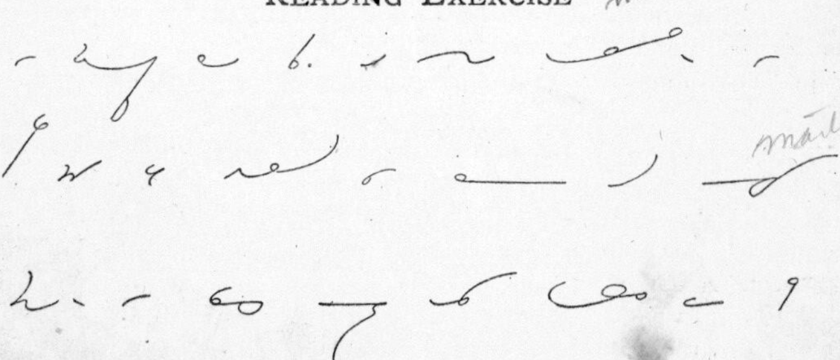

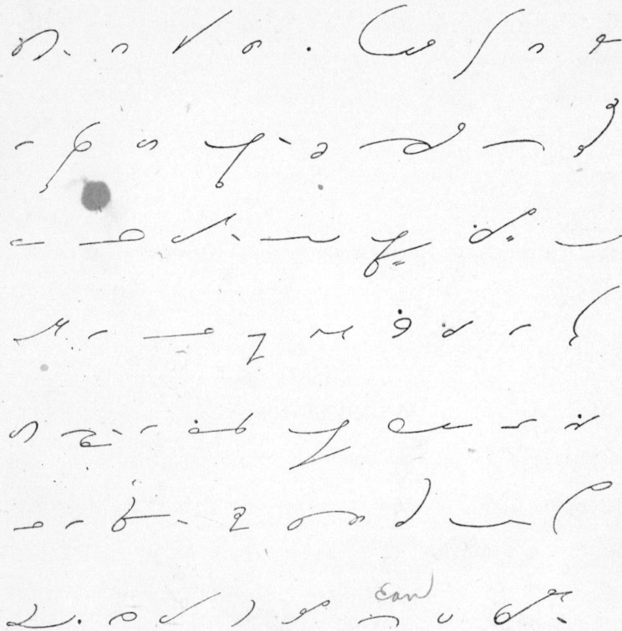

WRITING EXERCISE

1. The poems of Robert Burns portray his love for mankind, as shown in-the line "A man's a man for all that."

2. We-can-not fill your first order until we-have heard from-your references.

3. In-the northern territory this organization sells only to certain firms, but in-the southern cities it does a large mail order business.

4. The firm in-question deals in hardware and sells all styles of churns, hammers and other tools to-the farmers in-this and bordering countries.

NINTH LESSON

WORD-SIGNS

60. The forms on this page should be transcribed without referring to the key. Afterwards the student should compare his transcript with the key, and make corrections.

REVIEW EXERCISE ON WORD-SIGNS

KEY TO REVIEW EXERCISE ON WORD-SIGNS

61. The student should test his knowledge of the word-signs by writing the following words in shorthand, afterwards comparing the forms he has written with those given on the opposite page. In doing this it is a good plan to place a ring around any word incorrectly written, and afterwards write several lines of the correct form.

1. a-an, about, above, after, agent, all, allow, am-more, and-end, any, are-our, ask, assist.
2. at-it, attention, be-but-by, become-book, been-bound, before-behalf, behind, belief-believe, between, beyond, body, business, call, can.
3. care, cause-because, certificate, change-which, check, company-keep, could, course, date-did, definite, desire, determine.
4. devote, differ-ent-ence, difficult-y, duty, else-list, endure, ever-y, exist-ence, fall-follow, far-favor, find, firm, first.
5. for, form-from, friend-ly, full-y, gave, gentlemen, give-n, glad, go-good, great, hand.
6. have, he, how-out, I, in-not, inclose, instant-instance, is-his, judge, kind, let-letter, light, like.
7. little, long, look, market-Mr., Messrs., most, move, much, must.
8. name, new, next, of, one, order, organize-organization, other, particular, please, point-appoint, public-publish, put.
9. question, real-regard, receive, refer-ence, reply, represent, right-write, says-system, season, shall-ship, should, side, society, some.
10. soon, speak-speech, state, such, sure-ly, teach, territory, than-then, that, the, their-there, them, they, thing-think, this, those.
11. time, told, to-morrow, trust, until, upon, use, usual-ly-wish, very, want, was, week, well-will, went.
12. were, what, when, where, while, why, wife, wire, word, work, world, would, yes, you-your.

List of Additional Word-Signs

62. Many of these words are written in accordance with rules given at a later stage of the study, but are presented now so that the student may begin dictation on connected matter. As these words are of frequent occurrence, the forms should be diligently practiced, in order to gain facility in writing them.

accept-ance	bring
accord	capital
accordance	car, correct
acknowledge	carry
acquaint-ance	character
advantage	charge
advertise	clear-ly
again	clerk
agree	collect
always	consider-ation
arrange-ment	copy
avoid	corporation
beauty	correspond-ence
better	cover
bill	credit

custom
deliver
direct
dollar
draft
duplicate
during, Dr.
educate
effect
either
enough
experience
fault (see *fall*)
future
God
gone
got
govern-ment
house
immediate-ly

import-$^{ant}_{ance}$
improve-ment
industry
influence
insur-$^{e}_{ance}$
invoice
jury
mortgage
never
newspaper
object
oblige
occasion
occup-$^{y}_{ation}$
office
official
opinion
part
princip-$^{al}_{le}$
publication

pupil
quality
quantity
railroad
railway
recent
record
regret
remark
remit-tance
report
respect-ful-ly
return
satis-fy / satis-factory
satisfaction
send
signific-ant / signific-ance
sir
small

spirit
stand
stock
strange
strong, strength
suggest-ion
thank
thorough-ly, three
throughout
truth
typewriter
value
vowel
wealth (see *well*)
with
without
wonder
yesterday
young

NOTES: (a) The plural of word-signs ending in *S* is formed as follows:

causes | instances | respects

(b) To express the plural of word-signs ending in a circle and of some words ending in a loop, a slight change is made in the manner of joining S.

names | cares | carries

families | homilies | anomalies

(c) After a circle vowel, *ly* is written outside the preceding consonant, thus:

namely | dearly | likely

daily | nearly | merely

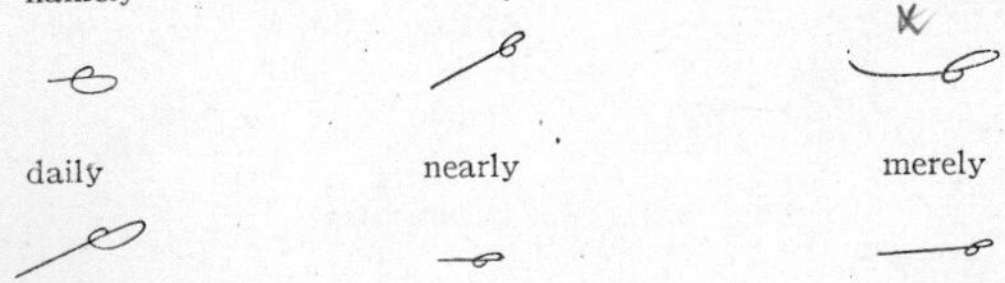

(d) *Ly* is added to words ending in the diphthong *i* by the double circle.

lightly | kindly | rightly

READING EXERCISE

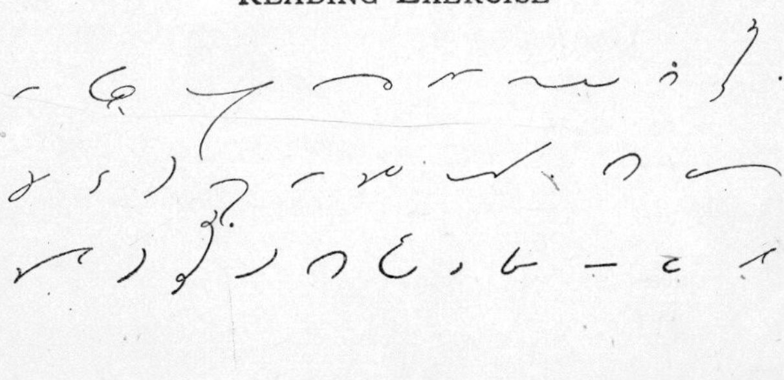

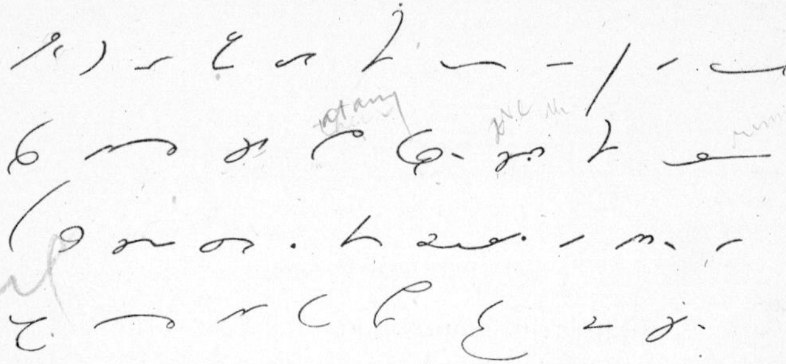

WRITING EXERCISE

1. The government will insure the goods against loss.
2. Your acceptance of our order is in accordance with the arrangement, a copy of which I gave to your clerk.
3. His long experience in writing advertising copy will be an advantage to the new official in his work with the insurance corporation.
4. Quality is more important than quantity. Your motto should be "Not how much, but how well."
5. The charge of the judge will oblige the jury to consider the character and occupation of the victim.
6. The agent reports that he could not send the book yesterday but that he will deliver it to-morrow without fail.
7. The typewriter is of great value in the business office. In truth it is difficult to do business without one.
8. He says that most of his pupils wish to take the full course and that he is planning the organization of a new class at the beginning of next month.
9. We suggest that the society arrange to take some action on this report and that such action be made a part of the record.
10. Please send a check with your next order or we cannot accord it immediate attention.
11. The report of this season's business is thoroughly satisfactory.
12. The object of this publication is to place before the public the truth about the recent report on the railway stock.

TENTH LESSON

Compound Words

63. A number of compounds may be obtained by joining simple word-signs, as illustrated in the second lesson by the word "before." The following words are formed on the same principle:

NOTE: Slight modifications or omissions are made in the forms for *anywhere, anyhow, hereinafter, herewith, however, sometime,* and *somewhere.* These should receive special attention. The form for *notwithstanding* is *not-with-s.*

Miscellaneous Compounds

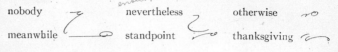

nobody	nevertheless	otherwise
meanwhile	standpoint	thanksgiving

KEY TO COMPOUND WORDS

any: anybody, anyone, anywhere, anyhow.

be: before, beforehand, behindhand, belong, beside.

ever-y: whatever, whenever, whichever, however, whoever, everybody, everyone, everywhere.

here: hereafter, herein, hereinafter, hereinbefore, hereon, hereto, heretofore, hereunto, herewith.

there: thereafter, therein, therefore, therefrom, thereon, thereto, thereupon, therewith.

where: whereabouts, whereas, wherever, wherefore, wherein, whereof, whereon, elsewhere.

soever: whatsoever, wheresoever, whensoever, whosoever, whomsoever.

some: somebody, somehow, someone, sometime, somewhat, somewhere.

with: within, withstand, forthwith, notwithstanding.

Derivatives, Etc.

64. After abbreviated words and words ending in a reversed circle, a short dash struck upward is used to express the past tense; the disjoined *r* expresses the terminations *er*, *or*, and the disjoined *ri*, expresses *ary*, *ory*.

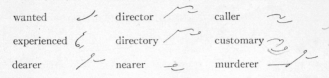

wanted	director	caller
experienced	directory	customary
dearer	nearer	murderer

NOTE: When the forms are distinctive, *er*, *or*, *ary*, *ory*, may be joined, as in *greater*, *boundary*, *receiver*, *stronger*, *writer*, *reporter*.

65. When a word-sign ends with the *last consonant of the word*, the reversing principle may be used to express *er* after straight lines.

sooner	longer	firmer	teacher

66. The word-signs *after* (*af*) and *out* (*ow*) may be used as prefix forms.

aftertimes	afternoon	outstanding	outside

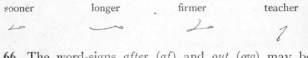

GENERAL EXERCISE

cared	collected	creditor
favored	corrected	fuller
returned	insured	giver
believed	insurer	kinder
caused	advertiser	recorder
inclosed	clearer	speaker

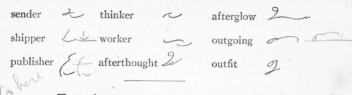

sender	thinker	afterglow
shipper	worker	outgoing
publisher	afterthought	outfit

THE ABBREVIATING PRINCIPLE

67. Many long words may be abbreviated by dropping the terminations. It would be a waste of time and effort to write more of a word than is necessary to suggest it when transcribing. This principle is already familiar in longhand, as *Rev.* for *Reverend*, *ans.* for *answer*, *Jan.* for *January*, *Phila.* for *Philadelphia*, etc.

The extent to which the principle may be applied depends upon the familiarity of the writer with the words and subject matter. Every writer can apply it easily and naturally to familiar words, and adapt it to the special requirements of the line of work in which he may be engaged.

The words given in this lesson are among the most common and useful illustrations of the application of this principle. When these have been studied, it will be easy to apply the principle in general practice. Many of the words given in subsequent lessons are abbreviated in this way. It is important to bear in mind that all the words so abbreviated will usually occur in sentences. For instance in the sentence "He was received with great enthusiasm," it would be sufficient to write *enthus* for *enthusiasm;* and the same form might be used for *enthusiastic* in "He met with a most enthusiastic reception."

ILLUSTRATION OF ABBREVIATING PRINCIPLE

It is *pos*sible that the *suc*cess of the *ma*gazine may

make it *necessary* to change the *pol*icy of the *asso*ciation

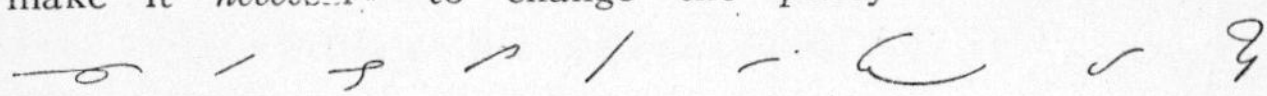

at the next meeting in *Phila*delphia sometime in *Jan*uary.

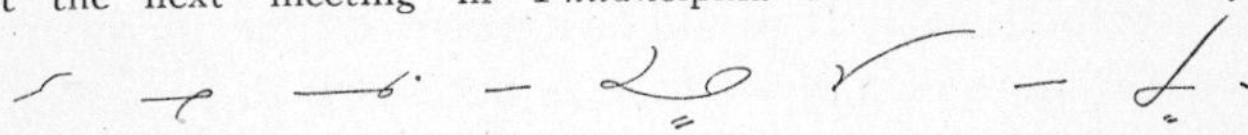

Have you a *memo*randum of their *finan*cial standing?

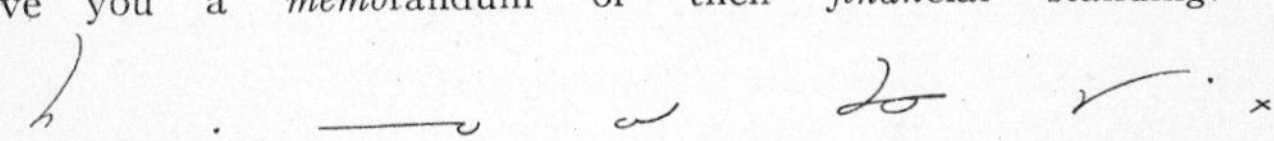

We cannot *canc*el the *bal*ance. The *Feb*ruary *num*ber will

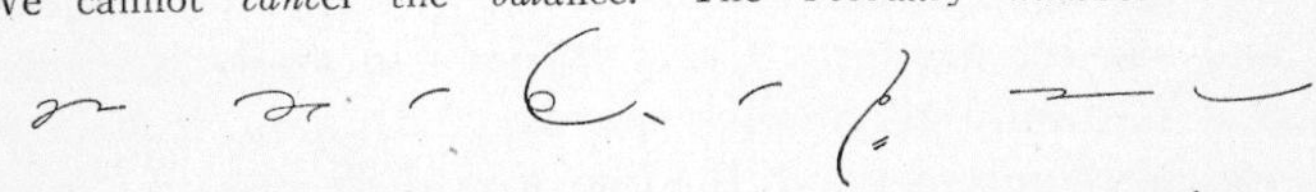

contain an *ori*ginal story by a very *promin*ent writer.

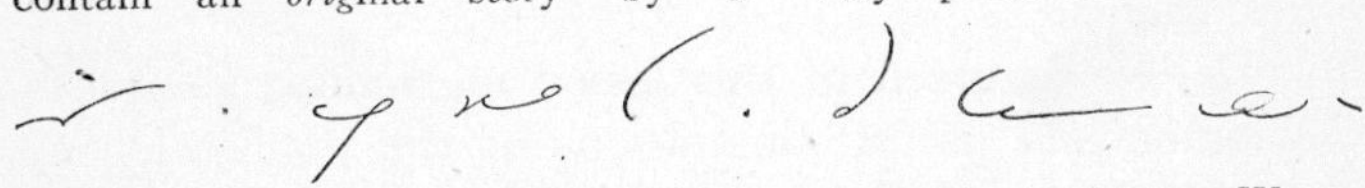

Please *ans*wer this letter before *Sep*tember first. We

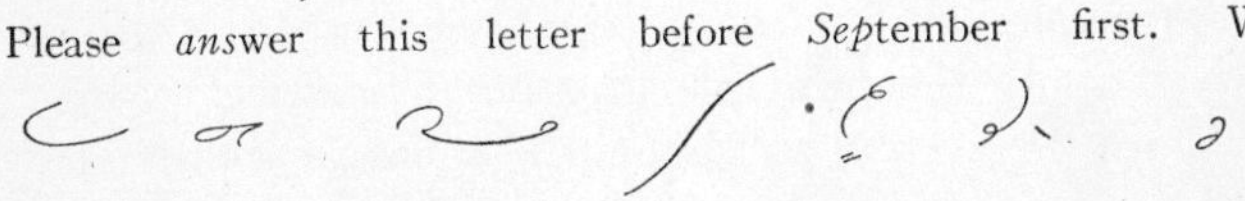

*remem*ber your *co-op*eration at that time and we shall show

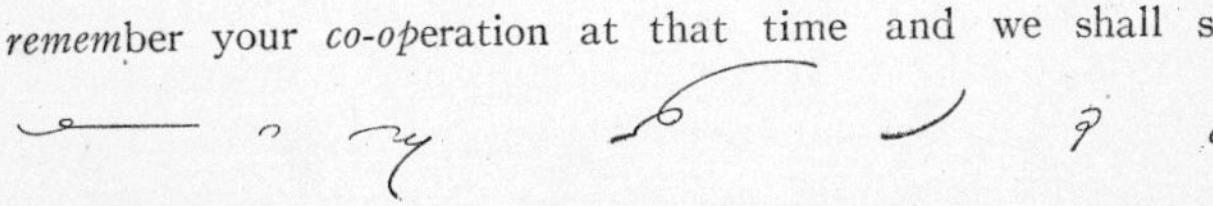

our *appre*ciation when there is an *oppor*tunity to do so.

Exercise on Abbreviating Principle

The following words are to be written in shorthand, and afterwards compared with the forms given on the opposite page:

1. aband(on), abbrev(iate), abs(ent), abso(lute), accus(tom), alph(abet), ambass(ador), anim(al), anon(ymous), ans(wer).
2. apol(ogize), apprec(iate), assoc(iation), attit(ude), attrib(ute), bal(ance), brill(iant), cal(culate), canc(el).
3. cap(able), Cath(olic), celeb(rate), chil(dren), collat(eral), conseq(uence), co-op(erate), deg(ree).
4. delib(erate), demons(trate), dict(ate), dilap(idate), dilig(ence), dis(count), eloq(uent), emin(ent).
5. Eng(land), enthus(iasm), entit(le), estab(lish), estim(ate), fam(iliar), finan(cial), freq(uent), gen(eral).
6. grat(itude), hund(red), inaug(urate), indic(ate), innoc(ence), invol(ve), irresis(tible), journ(al).
7. knowl(edge), lang(uage), leg(al), leng(th), lib(erty), loc(al), mag(azine).
8. mat(ter), melan(choly), memo(randum), mod(erate), neg(lect), negoti(ate), num(ber).
9. num(erous), obse(rve), obv(ious), oppor(tunity), ordin(ary), orig(inal), pamph(let), pecu(liar), pecun(iary), perman(ent).
10. perpend(icular), pleas(ant), pol(icy), pop(ular), pos(sible), pov(erty), predeces(sor), pref(er), prej(udice), prelim(inary).
11. prep(are), pres(ent), presi(de), priv(ilege), promin(ent), rath(er), relinq(uish), remem(ber).
12. remons(trate), rev(erend), ridic(ulous), scrup(ulous), separ(ate), sev(eral), simil(ar), simul(taneous), singu(lar).
13. splend(id), suc(cess), suf(ficient), synon(ymous), temp(erance), trav(el), unan(imous), un(ion), vul(gar).

Exercise on Abbreviating Principle

The following words are to be transcribed without referring to the key on the opposite page until the work has been completed.

1.
2.
3.
4.
5.
6.
7.
8.
9.
10.
11.
12.
13.

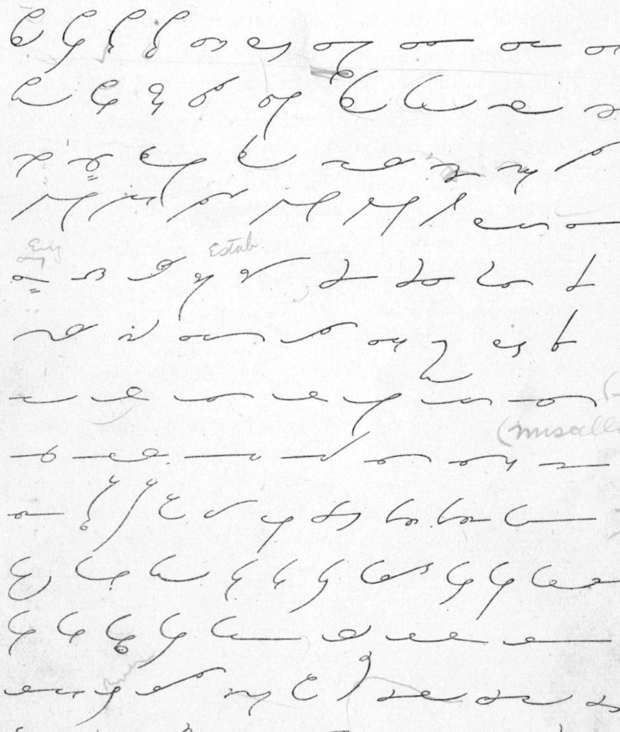

68. The Abbreviating Principle may be applied to a *short* word when a distinctive outline is secured. Usually this is done after a diphthong or strongly sounded vowel, as illustrated in the word-signs *right-write*, *find*, *light*, *side*. The following are useful examples:

bright	client	trade
delight	private	grade
arrive	trial	freight
derive	doubt	claim
decide	loyal-ty	poor
unite	power	cure
strike	proud	night
entire	thousand	to-night

Days and Months

Sunday	January	August
Monday	February	September
Tuesday	March	October
Wednesday	April	November
Thursday	May	December
Friday	June	
Saturday	July	

FIGURES, ETC.

69. After numerals the word *dollars* is expressed by *d; hundred* by *n* placed under the numeral; *thousand* by *th; million* by *m* placed on the line close to the numeral; *billion* by *b; pounds* (weight or money) by *p; gallons* by *g; barrels* by *br; bushels* by *bsh; feet* by *f; francs* by *fr; cwt* by *nw; o'clock* by *o* placed over the numeral:

$5	£5,000
500	£500,000
$500	five gallons
5,000	five barrels
$5,000	five bushels
500,000	five feet
5,000,000	five cwt.
$5,000,000	five o'clock
5 lbs. (or £5)	500 feet
500 lbs. (or £500)	five francs

70. These signs may be used after the article *a* and such words as *per, few, several:*

a dollar	few thousand dollars
a thousand dollars	a pound

a hundred thousand
several hundred
several hundred dollars

per hundred
a million
a gallon

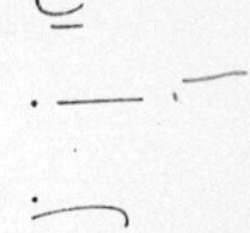

71. *Cents* when preceded by dollars may be expressed by writing the figures representing them very small and above the numerals for the dollars; when not preceded by dollars the sign for *s* is placed above the figures. *Per cent* is expressed by *s* written below the figures; *per cent per annum* by adding *n* to per cent.

$8.50 five cents five per cent five per cent per annum

Reading Exercise

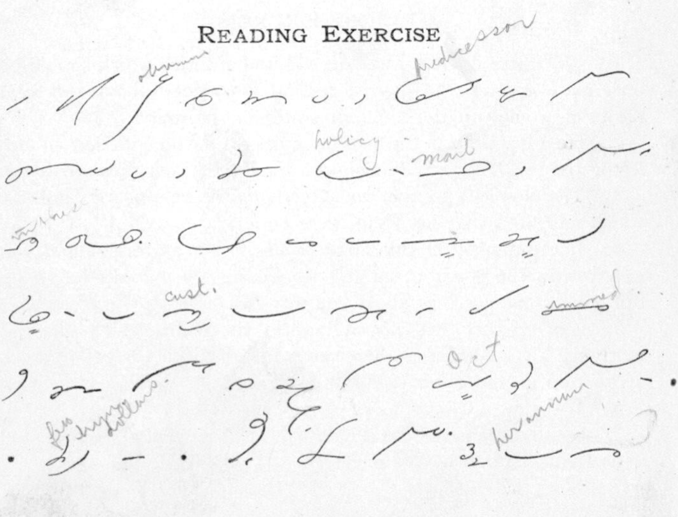

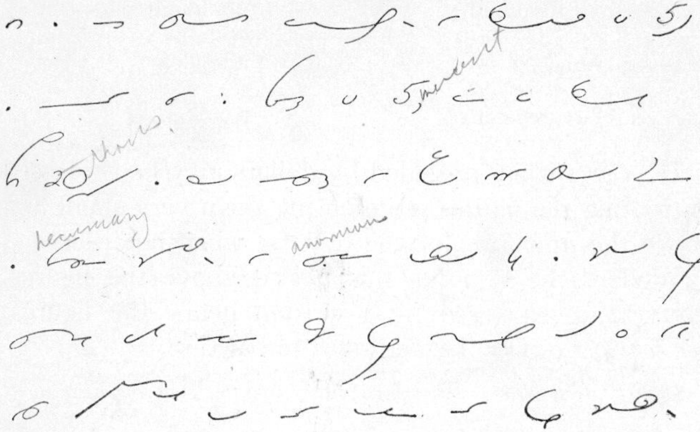

Writing Exercise

1. Elsewhere in this issue you will find a notice which should be read by everyone who desires general knowledge about the legal rights of women in the different states in the union.

2. He advertised in the afternoon papers for an experienced collector and by 10 o'clock that night a hundred replies were received.

3. The eloquent speaker was greeted with enthusiastic applause which indicated that his views were popular.

4. If the quality of this merchandise is not as represented you may return the goods to us and we will give you credit for them, but we cannot possibly allow you any discount on the balance.

5. The creditor will not relinquish the claim which his first mortgage gives him, and therefore we cannot sell the entire stock at auction as the other creditors suggested.

6. We allow a discount of 5% on cash sales.

7. Some customers take advantage of this even when they find it necessary to borrow the money.

ELEVENTH LESSON

PHRASE-WRITING

72. The student should cultivate the practice of joining small words, for without it great proficiency can never be attained. All the common phrases consisting of two or three words should be written with the same facility as an ordinary word-form, but nothing is gained by straining after special forms for uncommon phrases, or where the outline requires more than five efforts of the pen. While experience must ever be the supreme teacher in phrase-writing, the following suggestions will be useful.

(*a*) At the outset short and common words only should be joined.

(*b*) The words should make good sense if standing alone, as *I am glad.*

(*c*) The outlines for the words should be capable of being easily joined.

(*d*) Phrases that carry the hand away from the line of writing should be avoided; in other words, the writer should aim at onward movement.

(*e*) Pronouns are generally joined to the words they precede, as *I am, I shall, you can, we have.*

(*f*) A qualifying word may be joined to the word it qualifies, as *good men.*

(*g*) The prepositions *to, of, in* and *with,* and the conjunction *and* are generally joined to the words they precede, as *to have*, *of which*, *in case*, *with this*, and *there*.

(*h*) The auxiliary verbs *should*, *would*, *could* are generally joined to the words they precede, as *should be*, *would be*, *could be*.

In practicing the phrases given in this manual, the student should keep steadily in mind that they are given as *examples*, and that he is to form his own phrases on similar lines in general practice. He should study the phrases here given with a view of noting not only the nature of the joinings, but also the nature of the words that are joined.

General Exercise

it is	of our	I am
of the	of all	I can
to the	we are	I have
to this	from the	you have
in the	from you	I would
on the	which the	I will
of his	which is	you can
of their	which can	you will
of your	that the	of which
is the	there is	it was
in our	there are	in which

by the	all right	in this
by which	there were	in these
to you	there will	in those
for the	may be	in thus
for this	will be	I inclose
with the	would be	we inclose
with this	at hand	in regard

Word Modifications

Very useful and distinctive phrase-forms are obtained by modifying the forms for certain words.

73. Before words beginning with a downward character or O, R, L, *to* is expressed by *t*.

to be	to favor	to honor
to have	to please	to receive
to pay	to believe	to look

74. When repeated in a phrase, the word *as* is expressed by *s*:

as well as	as great as	as many as
as good as	as much as	as long as

75. In phrases *been* is expressed by *b:*

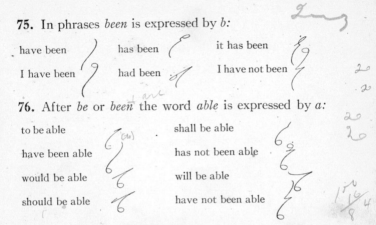

have been · has been · it has been

I have been · had been · I have not been

76. After *be* or *been* the word *able* is expressed by *a:*

to be able · shall be able

have been able · has not been able

would be able · will be able

should be able · have not been able

77. The following method of expressing *had* after pronouns should be carefully noted:

I had · they had · we had · you had

78. When *do not* is preceded by a pronoun, it is expressed by the sign for *dn.*

I do not · we do not

you do not · I do not think

they do not · you do not know

79. *Don't* is distinguished from *do not* by writing *dōn.*

I don't think · you don't know · I don't believe

80. The phrase *was not* may be easily and legibly expressed by writing *wasn't*, that is, by joining *s* to *nt* without an angle. For the same reason, *it is not* is written *it isn't* and *there is not* is written *there isn't*. If the contractions *wasn't*, *isn't* need to be clearly indicated, an apostrophe is placed over the forms.

it is not it was not he was not it wasn't

81. The words *ago*, *early*, *few*, *him*, *hope*, *sorry*, *want*, are modified as shown in the following phrase-forms:

weeks *ago*		to *him*	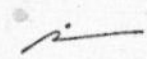
months ago		I told him	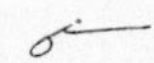
years ago		we told him	
at an *early* date		I *hope*	
at an early day		we hope	
early reply		I am *sorry*	
few days		we are sorry	
few days ago		I *want*	
few months		you want	
few months ago	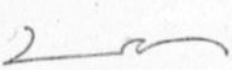	we want	
few minutes		if you want	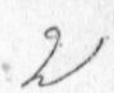
few minutes ago		do you want	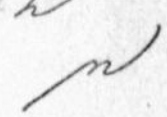

Omission of Words

82. The phrase *of the* may be omitted and its omission implied by writing the words it connects close together.

Your letter of the 4th inst. 

time of the day 

end of the week 

state of the market 

credit of the firm 

list of the people 

83. The words *from* and *to* are omitted in such phrases as *from time to time*.

from time to time 

from month to month 

from day to day 

from year to year 

from week to week 

from season to season 

84. The word *after* is omitted in such phrases as *day after day*, but the words are not joined.

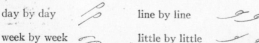

time after time 

week after week 

day after day 

month after month 

hour after hour 

year after year 

85. The word *by* is omitted in such phrases as *day by day*, the last word being written a little below the first word.

day by day 

line by line 

week by week 

little by little 

86. The word *to* is omitted after the words *able*, *according*, *glad*, *like*, *order*, *please*, *reference*, *regard*, *regret*, *relative*, *respect*, *wish*.

able to say		in reference to the matter	
in respect to the		glad to see	
in regard to the matter		I regret to say	
in reference to the		wish to say	

87. Any unimportant word may be omitted where the grammatical construction of the sentence would compel its restoration when transcribing.

in the world		some of them	
here and there		week or two	
more and more		son-in-law	

General Exercise

to see		*as* near *as*	
to ship		as low as	
to which		as soon as	
to reach		you have *been*	
to like		there has been	
to represent		what has been	
to sell		had been *able*	

will not be able

have you not been able

I had been

they had been

I *do not* see

I do not know

we do not know

I do not like

I *don't* see

there *was not*

days *ago*

ten days ago

for a *few* days

I *hope* to hear

I am *sorry* to say

if you *want* any

particulars *of the* work

cheer *after* cheer

side *by* side

on the question

day or two

in a day or two

in reply to your

ought to receive

out of the question

in a week or two

to-day or to-morrow

some of those

by the way

hand in hand

that is to say

system of government

form of government

one of our

one or two

one of the best

ought to be

ought to have

more or less

one of the most

to here

Write out

Special Business Phrases

(See Also Page 37)

Dear Sirs

Dear Mr.

My dear Sir

Yours sincerely

Yours very sincerely

Very sincerely

Very sincerely yours

Sincerely yours

Very respectfully

Cordially yours

Very cordially yours

I am in receipt

We are in receipt

I am in receipt of your favor

We are in receipt of your favor

I am in receipt of your letter

Reading Exercise

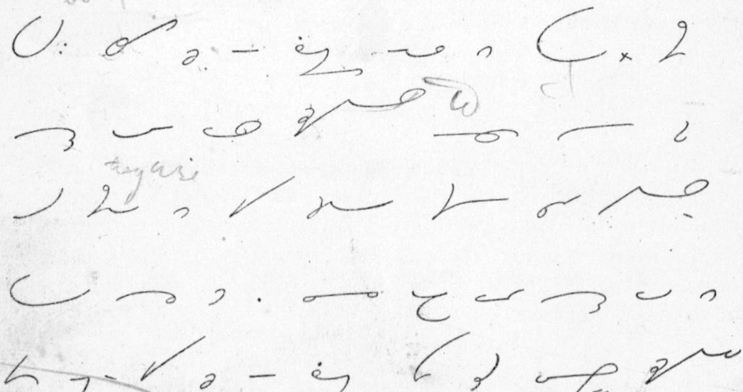

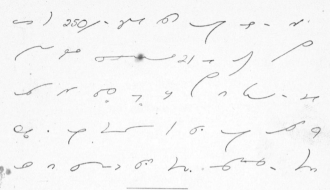

WRITING EXERCISE

1

Dear Madam:

We learn from your letter of May 10 that you are returning the books which we sent you a few months ago. You will be credited with these books when they reach us and the charge for them will be canceled. We are glad to know that you appreciate our courtesy in accepting their return. When you need anything more in our line, you will find us ever ready to serve you.

Very sincerely yours, (77)

2

Dear Sir:

We have your recent letter asking us to take advertising space in your newspaper. Our advertising plans for the next few months will not allow us to take any more newspaper space at this time. If you will bring this matter to our attention again in about three months, we may be able to arrange for a full page in the holiday issue to which you refer.

Very cordially yours, (72)

149

TWELFTH LESSON

Omission of Vowels

88. When two vowels not forming a pure diphthong come together, the minor or unaccented vowel may be omitted, and for convenience in writing many words the circle may be omitted in the diphthong *u*.

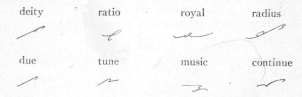

deity ratio royal radius

due tune music continue

89. In the body of a word short *u* and *ow* are omitted before *n*, *m*, *ng*, *nk*, *nt*, *nd*.

run come sun round

found rung sunk pungent

NOTES: (a) The short *u* is not omitted when it occurs between two horizontal straight strokes, as in *nun*, *numb*.

(b) The omission of *ow* between two horizontal straight strokes is indicated by the "jog" or broken line, as in *renown*, *announce*.

90. The vowel is omitted in the prefixes *be, de, re, dis, mis.*

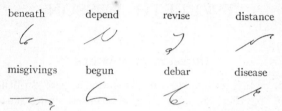

beneath | depend | revise | distance

misgivings | begun | debar | disease

NOTES: (a) The vowel is retained when *de* precedes K, G, as in *decay, degrade.*
(b) The vowel is retained when *re* precedes the forward characters, K, G, R, L, N, M, T, D, as in *recast, regain, rewrite, relate, renown, remiss, retail, redound.*

91. The vowel is omitted in *per, pur, pro,* and in the termination *age.*

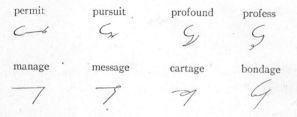

permit | pursuit | profound | profess

manage | message | cartage | bondage

NOTE: When *pro* occurs before an upward character or *K* — as in *protest, procrastinate*—it is more convenient to insert the vowel; when *per* occurs before an upward character — as in *perturb, pertain, perdition* — the reversing principle expresses R.

92. The vowels *ŭ, o͞o* are omitted after R or L when followed by Sh, Ch, J.

rush | flush | solution | drudge

93. The vowel is omitted in the terminations *tition, tation, dition, dation, nition, nation, mission, mation.*

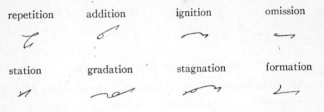

repetition addition ignition omission

station gradation stagnation formation

General Principles

94. While the omission of vowels in general is left to a very large extent to the judgment of the writer, the following suggestions will be of assistance:

(*a*) A vowel is often omitted between two reverse curves.

maker struck skill scarce

attract eager secure gulf

(*b*) A hook vowel is often omitted between T, D, R, L, and P, B.

stop drop Dublin adoption

(*c*) A circle vowel is often omitted between P, B, and a horizontal or upward character.

pity rapid open bad

Omission of Consonants

95. D is omitted when it immediately precedes M or V.

admit administer adverb advocate

NOTE: In the words *admire, advise, advance,* coming under this rule, the initial vowel may be omitted. This enables the writer to form such useful phrases as *I admire, we admire, to advise, I advise, we advise, to advance, in advance.*

96. When slightly enunciated, T or D is omitted at the end of a word.

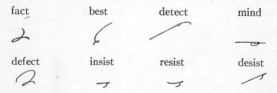

fact best detect mind

defect insist resist desist

97. The combination *ld* is expressed by raising the end of L.

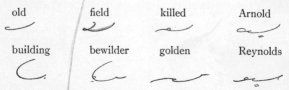

old field killed Arnold

building bewilder golden Reynolds

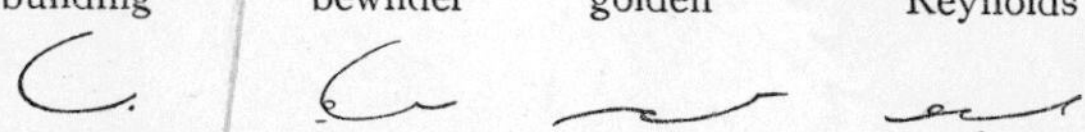

General Exercise

arduous
genius
genuine
astute
musician
virtue
theory
museum
harmonious
ceremonious
fun
lunch
column
front
brown
drown
sound
surround
foundry

astound
redound
mountainous
surmount
renounce
announce
legion
rejoice
review
repent
respond
replace
reside
resort
resource
begrudge
bequeath
betray
beseech

deserve
debase
debate
decision
discharge
disarm
discern
distort
discard
misprint
misquote
misguide
perhaps
permission
promotion
prolong
propel
provide
proper

sausage	tradition	pithy
dotage	foundation	apathy
passage	ammunition	carpet
damage	fascination	homeopathy
baggage	nomination	happen
package	assassination	facile
average	determination	normal
crush	domination	formal
blush	animation	vernal
resolution	estimation	mental
dissolution	occur	dental
visitation	currency	mortal
citation	sugar	actual
dictation	career	mutual
agitation	massacre	habitual
ostentation	equal	perpetual
hesitation	accuracy	amateur
recitation	carbon	torture
imitation	augur	picture
edition	epithet	creature

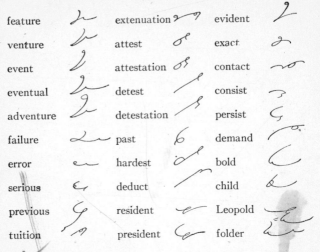

feature	extenuation	evident
venture	attest	exact
event	attestation	contact
eventual	detest	consist
adventure	detestation	persist
failure	past	demand
error	hardest	bold
serious	deduct	child
previous	resident	Leopold
tuition	president	folder

98. The following words coming under the rules given in this lesson are also useful illustrations of the Abbreviating Principle.

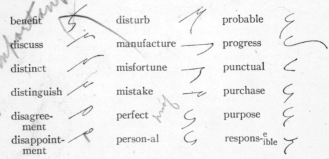

benefit	disturb	probable
discuss	manufacture	progress
distinct	misfortune	punctual
distinguish	mistake	purchase
disagreement	perfect	purpose
disappointment	person-al	respons-e, ible

NOTE: In *disagree, disappoint* and their derivatives, it is found convenient to write *d* for *dis.*

Very Important

special
off, offer
except

Reading Exercise

Writing Exercise

1. The theory was advanced that a solution of the bewildering mystery could be found only by following up every clue.

2. A special meeting was announced for the purpose of discussing the formation of a society for the benefit of the metal workers in the foundry.

3. Much damage was done to the baggage through rough handling and one package was entirely crushed.

4. Silence about the details of your office work is a virtue. The repetition of an innocent remark has often caused the failure of an important business deal.

5. The manager soon found there were profound misgivings about the outcome of the expedition.

THIRTEENTH LESSON

Joined Prefixes

99. Most of the joined prefixes are already familiar to the student. They are repeated at this time for the purpose of furnishing sufficient practice to eliminate hesitation in using them in actual work.

100. Al, expressed by *aw*; and **Ul,** by *u*.

almost also ultimo (ult.) ulcer

101. Com, Con, Coun, Cog, expressed by *k*.

competition confess counsel cognomen

Notes: (a) Before *t* or *d* the prefix form may express *can*.

cantaloupe candidate candor candle

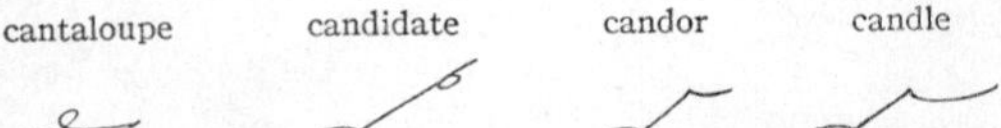

(b) When Com or Con is followed by a vowel or by *r* or *l*, write *km* for *com* and *kn* for *con*.

comedy comrade conic Conroy

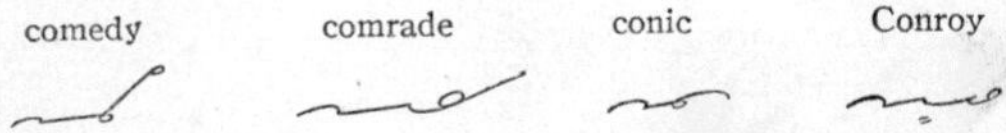

102. Em, Im, expressed by *m*; and **En, In, Un,** by *n*.

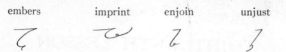

embers imprint enjoin unjust

103. (*a*) The prefix forms for *em*, *im*, *en*, *in*, *un* are used only when a consonant follows the prefix. When a vowel follows *em*, *im*, *en*, *in*, *un*, the initial vowel is written.

emit innate inner inept

enact unequal imagine inaccessible

(*b*) Negative words beginning with *im*, *un* are distinguished from the positive forms by the insertion of the initial vowel.

Positive

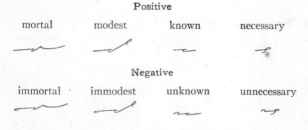

mortal modest known necessary

Negative

immortal immodest unknown unnecessary

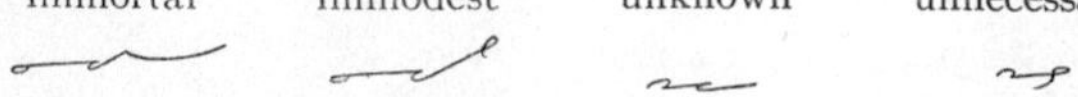

104. Ex, expressed by *es*; **Aux** and **Ox,** by *os*.

exceed expel auxiliary oxygen

105. **For, Fore, Fur,** expressed by *f*.

forgive foresight furnish forearm

NOTE: When **For** or **Fore** is followed by a vowel, disjoin *f* and write the next character close to it, as in *forearm*. When *For* or *Fore* is followed by *r* or *l*, form an angle after *f*, as in *forerunner*, *furlong*, page 92.

106. **Sub,** expressed by *s*.

subdue subpoena submit substance

NOTES: (a) Before R, L, Ch, J, or a hook, *s* is written contrary to rule to express *sub*.

sublime subjoin subway subordinate

(b) When **Sub** is followed by a circle vowel, *s* is disjoined and the next character is written close to it.

subeditor subagent subhead subequal

GENERAL EXERCISE

almanac		ulster	
although		compel	
ulterior	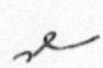	common	
ultimate		comprehend	
ultimatum		combine	

seven limits

commence
commission
commotion
commutation
comity
comatose
conceit
contest
concur
concussion
conditionally
confirm
consign
confound
consolation
consolidation
consternation
conduce
consummate
convince

convene
consul
conscious
cognate
embrace
emperor
impartial
imperfect
impossible
impulse
impoverish
impression
engine
encourage
ensign
enchant
infirm
invent
invest
investigate

unkind	fortune
uncouth	forsake
unlearned	foreground
emerge	forerunner
emotion	furlong
inhabit	forenoon
immersion	furnace
inaction	further
uneasy	furthermore
unnoticed	furthermost
expert	furtive
excess	furniture
exaggerate	forehead
excite	foreordain
excursion	subside
exhaust	subsequent
explosion	sublease
exhibit	suburb
oxalic	subsist
oxidize	subacid

COMPOUND JOINED PREFIXES

107. Two or more simple prefixes may be joined to form compounds. A few compounds may be formed by joining *re*, *dis*, *mis*, or *non* to the prefix forms:

incontestable
unconquerable
unaccounted*
incognito
incandescent
unimpaired*
uninitiated*
inexpensive*
insubordinate
inform
conform
comfort
unfortunate
unforeseen
encompass
inexpedient*
inexplicable*
excommunicate
inconvenient
inconsistent
disconcert
discontinue
preconcerted
misconduct
recompense
reconcile
recognize
recommend
noncontent
subconscious

*The initial vowel is not required because the word begins with a compound prefix.

writing exercises for lessons for Lessons 8-9-10. count as 1 page

PREFIXAL ABBREVIATIONS

108. The following are useful abbreviations under rules given in this and in previous lessons:

accomplish	economy
afford	effort
already	enable*
altogether	unable*
command	energy
commerce	excel-lent / -lence
commercial	except
committee	exchange
communicat-e / -ion	exercise
compare	expect
complete (complaint)	explain
conclude	express
conclusion	force
(comfort) confiden-t / -ce	indeed
congress	independen-t / -ce
connect	individual
country	subject

*See suffix *able*, page 109.

together profit broker
gather property

Reading Exercise

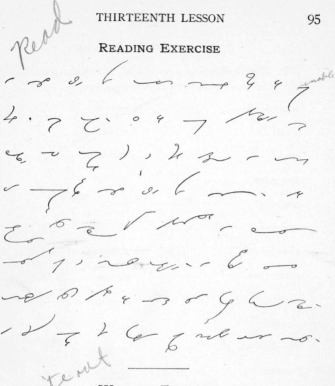

Writing Exercise

1. "The world will little note nor long remember what we say here, but it can never forget what they did here."

2. It needs no prophet to tell us that those who live up to their means without any thought of a reverse in life can never attain pecuniary independence.

3. To the cost of manufacturing and shipping add the profit of the manufacturer and that of the shipper—these items make up the price paid by the ultimate purchaser.

FOURTEENTH LESSON

THE TR PRINCIPLE

109. Certain prefixes or letters are disjoined to express *tr* and a following vowel. The prefix is placed above the line and very close to the remainder of the word, which rests on the line of writing.

Contr- (or *counter*)	contract	counteract
Constr-	construct	constraint
Extr- **Excl-** (or *exter*)	extract	exclamation
Intr- (or *inter, enter, intel*)	intricate	intellect
Instr-	instruct	instrument
Retr-	retract	retrograde
Restr-	restrict	restraint
Detr-	detract	detriment
Distr-	distract	distribute
Electr- (or *electric*)	electric	electric car
Alter	altercate	alternative
Ultra	ultra-violet	ultramarine

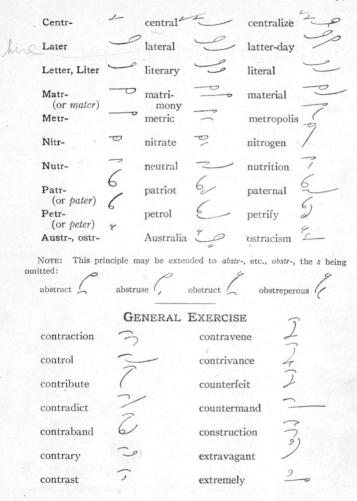

Centr-	central	centralize
Later	lateral	latter-day
Letter, Liter	literary	literal
Matr- (or *mater*)	matrimony	material
Metr-	metric	metropolis
Nitr-	nitrate	nitrogen
Nutr-	neutral	nutrition
Patr- (or *pater*)	patriot	paternal
Petr- (or *peter*)	petrol	petrify
Austr-, ostr-	Australia	ostracism

NOTE: This principle may be extended to *abstr-*, etc., *obstr-*, the *s* being omitted:

abstract abstruse obstruct obstreperous

GENERAL EXERCISE

contraction	contravene
control	contrivance
contribute	counterfeit
contradict	countermand
contraband	construction
contrary	extravagant
contrast	extremely

extradition
extraneous
extraordinary
external
exclude
exclusive
internal
interest
introduce
intervene
intelligent
intelligence
entertain
enterprise
international
interpret
intersect
interrupt
interview
instruction

retrieve
retrospect
retraction
retribution
restrain
restriction
deterioration
distraction
distress
distrust
electricity
electrician
electrotype
electric light
alteration
alternation
centrifugal
literature
liturgy
letterpress

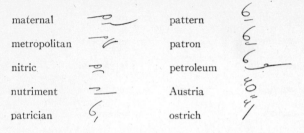

maternal	pattern
metropolitan	patron
nitric	petroleum
nutriment	Austria
patrician	ostrich

COMPOUND DISJOINED PREFIXES

110. Some very useful compounds are obtained by joining simple syllables, such as *un*, *in*, *dis*, *re*, *non*, to disjoined prefixes.

uncontradicted	unconstrained
uncontrolled	inextricable
incontrovertible	uninteresting
unrestrained	reconstruction
redistribution	misinterpret
disinterested	illiterate
uninterrupted	eccentric
unintelligent	concentration
unintellectual	nonintervention
indestructible	unalterable
immaterial	compatriot

Derivatives of Words Ending in CT

111. In forming the derivatives of words ending in *ct*, as *contract*, it is not necessary to disjoin to express *ed*, *or*, *er*, or *ive*. The *t* is omitted in the primitive form (under the rule given in Par. 96), and also its derivatives.

contracted	restrictive
contractor	unretracted
contractive	detracted
constructed	active
constructor	effected
constructive	effective
instructed	affected
instructor	defective
instructive	detected
extracted	detective

Reading Exercise

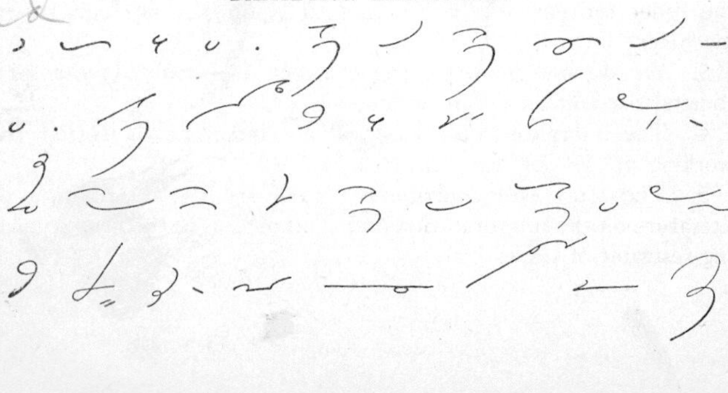

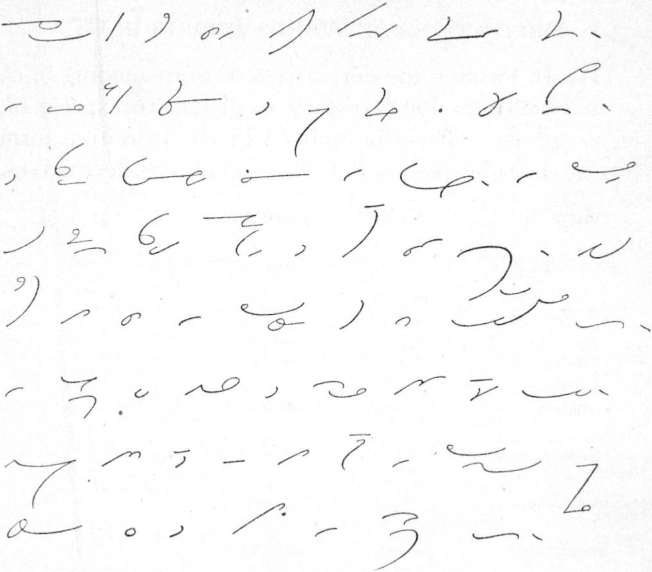

WRITING EXERCISE

1. The enterprise is international in its appeal and should be of extraordinary interest to the intelligent people of every land.

2. At the close of the interview the president countersigned the order for new electric motors to equip all the high power machines.

3. We do not interpret the contract as permitting our customers to countermand their orders.

4. The international society will not intervene to restrict the working of the new extradition laws.

5. The trust will contribute a fund for the distribution of literature on the interpretation and construction of the laws regarding restraint of trade.

FIFTEENTH LESSON

Disjoined Prefixes—continued

112. Aggra-e-i, expressed by loop *a*; and **Anta-e-i,** by circle *a*.

aggravate aggregate antagonist antipathy

113. Incli-e-u, expressed by *ĭ* (small circle).

incline inclemency include inclusive

114. Decla-i, expressed by *de*; and **Recla-i**, by *re*.

declare decline reclaim recline

Note: On account of the distinctive character of the form, **Decla-i** may be expressed without disjoining; thus

declare decline declaration declaim

115. Hydra-o, expressed by *ī* (diphthong ī).

hydrant hydraulic hydropathy hydrophobia

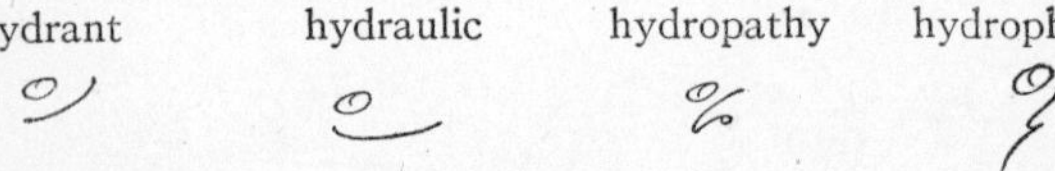

116. Magna-e-i (or Mc), expressed by *m*; and **Multi,** by *mu*.

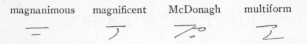

magnanimous magnificent McDonagh multiform

NOTE: When a distinction is required between **Mc** and **Mac,** write the stroke double length for **Mac.**

117. Over, expressed by *o*; and **Under,** by *u*.

overdue overthrow understand underneath

118. Para, expressed by *p*; and **Post,** by *p* (on the line, close to the next character).

parasite parallel postman postal

119. Self, Circu-m, expressed by *s* (to the left).

selfish self-esteem circulation circumvent

120. Super, Supre, expressed by *s* ("comma S").

superlative supreme superficial supervise

121. Short or **Ship,** expressed by *sh*; and **Trans,** by *t*.

shorthand shipwreck transaction translation

122. **Suspi, Suspe, Suscep,** expressed by *ses.*

suspicion suspense susceptible suspect

General Exercise

aggrieve	hydrogen
aggregation	hydrocarbon
agriculture	magnet
aggression	magnesia
aggressive	magnify
antidote	McKenzie
anticipate	MacIntosh
antecedent	McDougall
antediluvian	multitude
antithesis	multiply
declamation	overtake
declined	overbalance
reclined	overcharge
inclined	overlook
inclination	overcome
inclusion	overestimate

underscore
undertake
underwrite
undercurrent
paramount
paraphrase
paragraph
paradise
paragon
parapet
postage
postpone
post-office
postal card
self-evident
self-conscious
self-sufficient
self-improvement
circular
circumference
circumstance
superabundant
supercilious
superfine
supremacy
superfluous
superior
superintend
suppress
superb
shortcomings
shipshape
suspension
suspend
transfer
transition
transitory
transformation
transcend
transport

COMPOUND DISJOINED PREFIXES

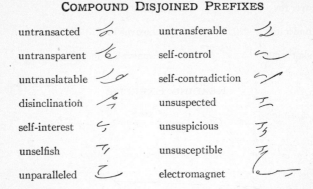

untransacted		untransferable	
untransparent		self-control	
untranslatable		self-contradiction	
disinclination		unsuspected	
self-interest		unsuspicious	
unselfish		unsusceptible	
unparalleled		electromagnet	

123. The words *misunderstand* and *misunderstood* are expressed by *stand* and *stood* placed under *mis*, with *mis* placed on the line of writing. This is extended to *understand* and *understood* when preceded by a pronoun, a wordsign or a short phrase form.

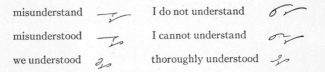

misunderstand		I do not understand	
misunderstood		I cannot understand	
we understood		thoroughly understood	

124. The words *extra*, *enter*, *over*, *under*, *short*, *alter*, *center*, *counter*, *construe*, *agree*, *deter*, are expressed by the prefixal forms placed over the next word.

extra discount		center rail	
enter into		counter claim	

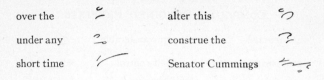

over the — alter this
under any — construe the
short time — Senator Cummings

READING EXERCISE

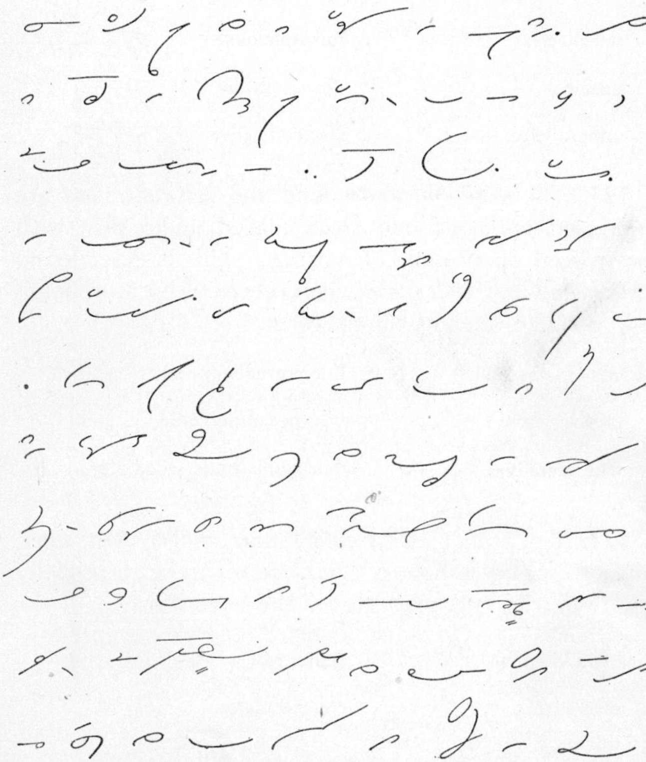

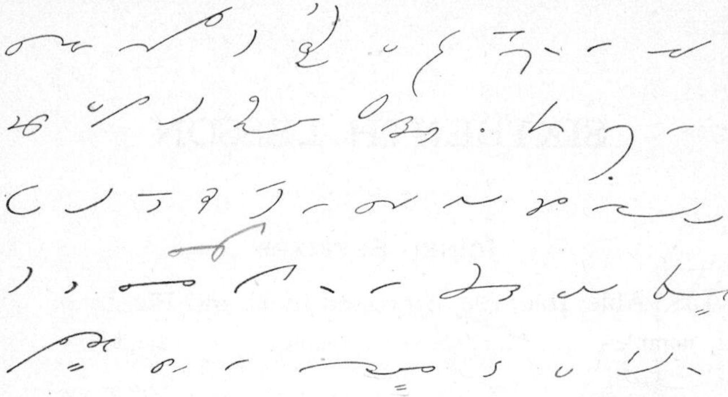

WRITING EXERCISE

1. Self-knowledge, self-reverence, self-control, these three alone lead men to supreme power.

2. It was our understanding that Doctor MacChesney was to translate that discussion on the transplanting of magnolia trees for the next issue of the Agricultural Review.

3. The extra discount allowed on the bill for goods purchased at the regular counter was not according to the new contract in which we agree to make a special price only on sales amounting to more than $200.

4. The circulation of the magazine is over fifty thousand without taking into account the extra copies sent out as exchanges.

5. It was self-evident that coal would be recognized as a contraband of war.

6. There was a general suspicion that his antagonist was a man of great intelligence and magnetism.

7. This system of shorthand is the very antithesis of the antiquated methods, and it is easy to demonstrate that it is vastly superior to any of them because there is a superabundance of evidence in its favor.

SIXTEENTH LESSON

JOINED SUFFIXES

125. **Able, Ible, Ble,** expressed by *b*; and **Ple,** by *p*.

notable — audible — noble — ample

126. **Cribe,** expressed by *kr*; and **Cription,** by *kr-shun*.

describe — description — prescribe — prescription

127. **Flect, Flict,** expressed by *fl*; and **Flection, Fliction,** by *fl-shun*.

afflict — affliction — reflect — reflection

128. **Ful,** expressed by *f*; **Less,** by *l*; **Ment,** by *m*; and **Ness,** by *n*.

thoughtful — artless — amusement — lateness

NOTES: (a) When *ment* is preceded by a *vowel*, it is generally advisable to write the word in full.

cement — raiment — lament — foment

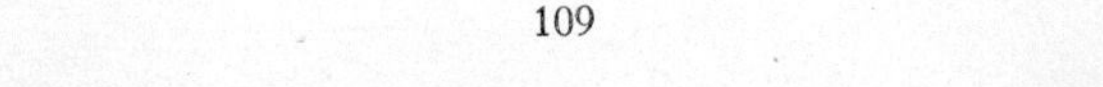

(b) Where the root word is abbreviated to one character, *ness* is written in full, as in the word *goodness*, which is written *g-n-e-s*. If the primitive word, although a word-sign, is more fully suggested, the suffix form is used.

fullness littleness gladness friendless

(c) An angle is formed in joining *ness* where the absence of an angle would give the form of a different word.

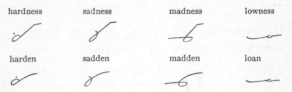

hardness sadness madness lowness

harden sadden madden loan

129. Pose, expressed by *po*; **Position,** by *po-shun*; **Pute,** by *pu*; and **Putation,** by *pu-shun*.

impose imposition impute imputation

130. Pire, expressed by *pī*; and **Quire,** by *kī*.

aspire inspire conspire respire

acquire inquire require esquire

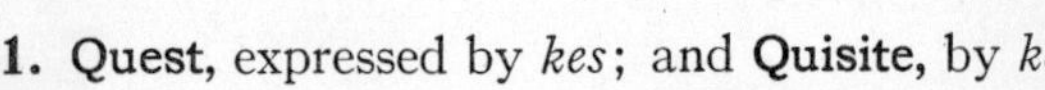

131. Quest, expressed by *kes*; and **Quisite,** by *kest*.

request conquest requisite exquisite

132. Self, expressed by *s*; and **Selves,** by *ses.*

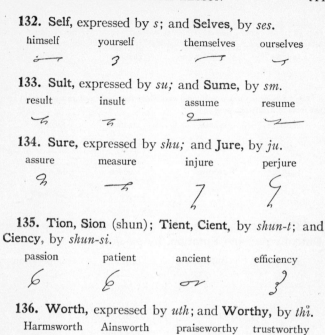

himself yourself themselves ourselves

133. Sult, expressed by *su;* and **Sume,** by *sm.*

result insult assume resume

134. Sure, expressed by *shu;* and **Jure,** by *ju.*

assure measure injure perjure

135. Tion, Sion (shun); **Tient, Cient,** by *shun-t*; and **Ciency,** by *shun-si.*

passion patient ancient efficiency

136. Worth, expressed by *uth*; and **Worthy,** by *thi̊.*

Harmsworth Ainsworth praiseworthy trustworthy

General Exercise

suitable
peaceable
horrible
salable

eatable
irritable
payable
humble

nimble
readable
seasonable
admissible
admirable
laudable
assignable
attainable
terrible
pliable
interminable
tangible
formidable
incomparable
endurable
traceable
credible
trouble
sample
example

simple
transcribe
transcription
inscribe
inscription
conflict
confliction
inflict
infliction
handful
bashful
useful
watchful
wonderful
successful
aimless
fearless
homeless
breathless
thoughtless

wireless
moment
defacement
ornament
augment
achievement
appointment
experiment
investment
comment
bareness
rudeness
fairness
slowness
expose
exposition
suppose
supposition
oppose
opposition

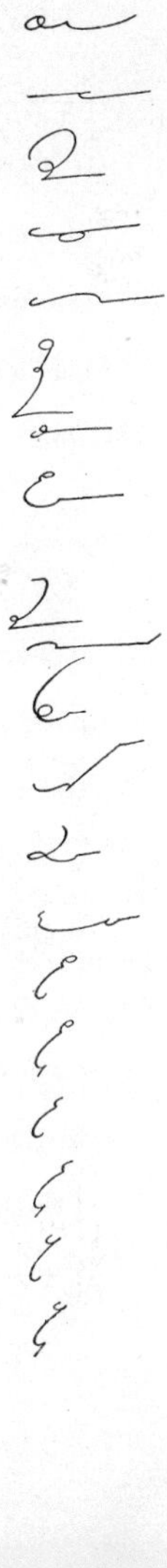

propose
proposition
proposal
depose
deposition
dispose
disposition
disposal
decompose
repute
reputation
compute
computation
depute
deputation
dispute
disputation
transpire
expire
myself

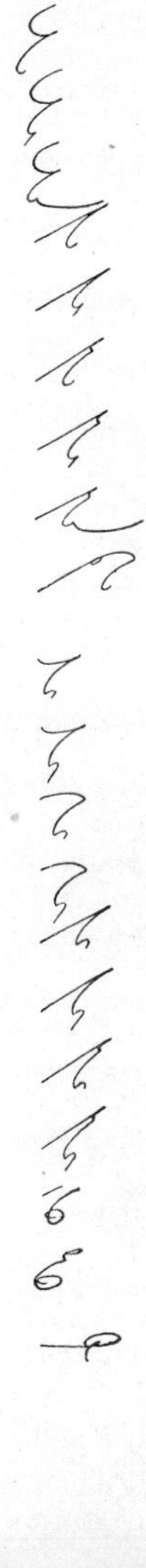

yourselves
consult
desultory
consume
leisure
treasure
censure
pressure
adjure
conjure
efficient
deficient
deficiency
proficient
proficiency
Ellsworth
blameworthy
noteworthy

COMPOUND JOINED SUFFIXES

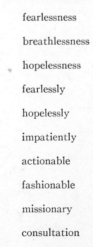

feebleness
hopefulness
thoughtfulness
playfulness
carefulness
hopefully
thoughtfully
playfully
heedlessness
thoughtlessness
fearlessness
breathlessness
hopelessness
fearlessly
hopelessly
impatiently
actionable
fashionable
missionary
consultation

indescribable
measurable
immeasurable
requirement
acquirement
momentary
supplementary
elementary
complimentary
trustworthiness

READING EXERCISE

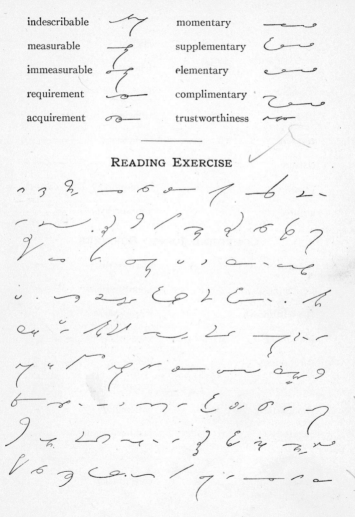

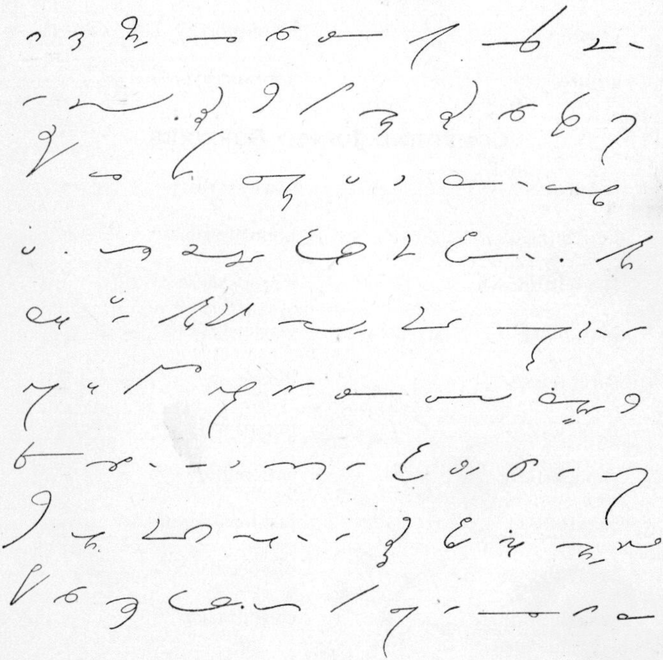

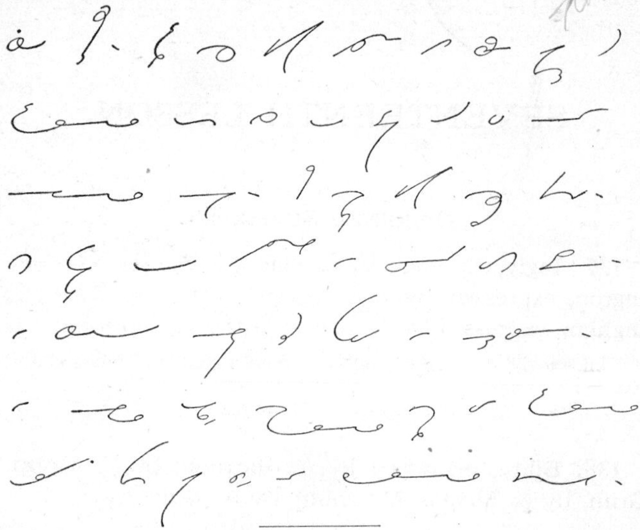

WRITING EXERCISE

1. His reading was desultory and therefore without result.

2. The achievement is so remarkable that it is almost incredible, but the truth of the report is vouched for by several reliable people.

3. After careful investigation they came to a decision that the additional loans would be too large an investment for the company to undertake with the capital at its disposal at that time.

4. The shorthand notes are legible, but the transcription is not acceptable because of the lack of neatness in the work.

5. The missionary underwent indescribable torture with a fearlessness which evoked the admiration of the savages.

6. The contribution is praiseworthy for its direct treatment of the subject, but it is not suitable for use in our publication and we are therefore returning it to you.

SEVENTEENTH LESSON

DISJOINED SUFFIXES

137. Ingly, expressed by *ly*, placed in the *ing* position; **Ington,** expressed by *ton*, placed in the *ing* position; **Ingham,** expressed by *m*, placed in the *ing* position.

knowingly Washington Kensington Dillingham

138. Bility, expressed by *b*; **Ification,** by *f*; **Gram, Grim,** by *g*; **Mental, Mentality,** by *m*; **Ship,** by *sh*.

ability feasibility specification monogram

experimental fundamental partnership ownership

NOTES: (a) After *t* and *d*, *ification* may be joined, as the absence of the blend clearly shows that *f* is a suffix sign.

modification notification edification ratification

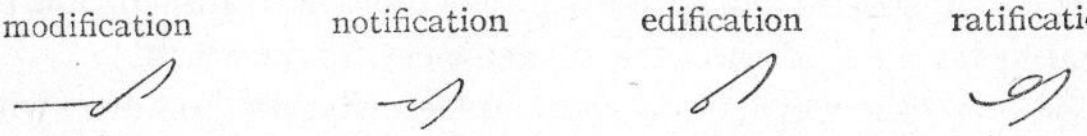

(b) In many words *ship* may be joined.

friendship workmanship hardship authorship

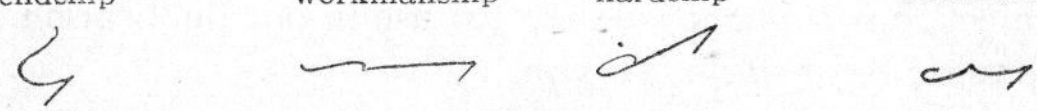

139. Hood or Ward, expressed by *d*.

childhood likelihood homeward downward

NOTE: In many words *ward* may be joined.

forward afterwards towards backward

140. Acle, Ical, Icle, expressed by *k*.

tentacle medical classical chronicle

141. Itis, expressed by *ts*.

appendicitis meningitis peritonitis tonsillitis

142. Ulate, expressed by *u*. In forming derivatives, the other letters are added.

modulate modulated insulate insulator

insulation formulate emulate emulative

NOTE: In most words *ulate* and its derivatives may be joined with perfect safety.

speculated speculation speculator speculative

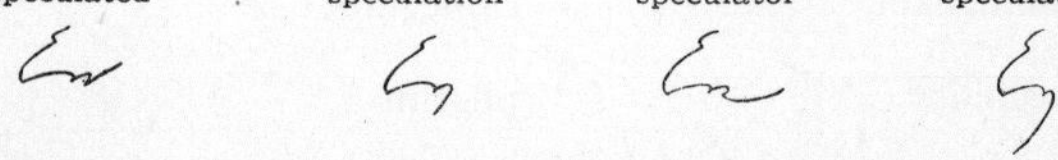

General Exercise

willingly
appallingly
strikingly
meaningly
soothingly
warningly
pleadingly
cheeringly
longingly
exceedingly
grudgingly
Millington
Farmington
Warrington
Wellington
Harrington
Rockingham
Cunningham
plausibility

nobility
sensibility
advisability
legibility
desirability
affability
qualification
gratification
signification
classification
mortification
indemnification
identification
certification
lettergram
phraseogram
epigram
cablegram
pilgrim

anagram
sentimental
ornamental
monumental
clerkship
apprenticeship
airship
township
steamship
kinship
warship
worship
womanhood
manhood
girlhood
boyhood
hardihood
motherhood
brotherhood
neighborhood

livelihood
knighthood
statehood
onward
upward
northward
southward
eastward
westward
awkward
reward
article
clerical
physical
psychical
musical
icicle
radical
technical
cuticle

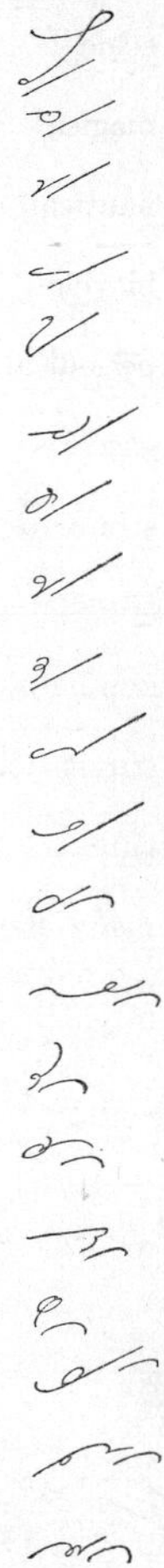

ethical
magical
nautical
bicycle
periodical
gastritis
stimulate
stimulated
stipulate
stipulation
cumulative
manipulate
manipulation
populated
articulate
articulation
inarticulate
formulated
adulation
expostulate
regulate
matriculate
perambulate
speculate

READING EXERCISE

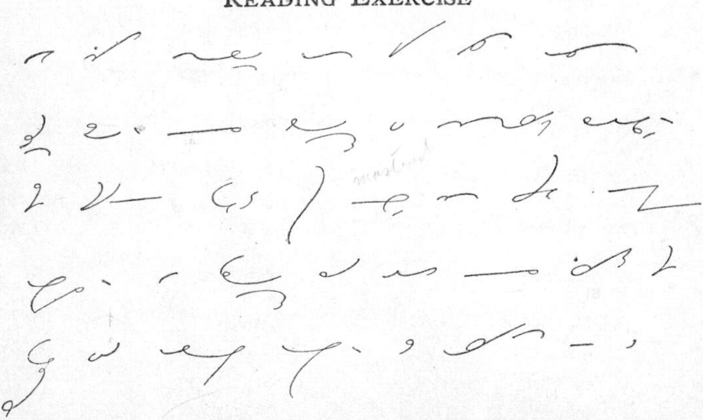

WRITING EXERCISE

1. The classification and identification of the candidates proved to be an exceedingly difficult task.

2. If you have the essential educational qualifications, we can easily arrange for the certification.

3. The technical nature of the matter makes the work of the medical reporter very difficult.

4. An article on psychical research appeared in a recent issue of the periodical.

5. Every girl, when she reaches womanhood, should be prepared to earn her own livelihood even though there is no likelihood of her being called upon to do so.

6. You may matriculate in the college when you receive a notification of your eligibility.

7. The articles of co-partnership were drawn up according to the specifications.

8. The law stipulated that the statement of ownership should be published every six months.

EIGHTEENTH LESSON

DISJOINED SUFFIXES—CONTINUED

143. -Rity, -Lity, -City, -Vity, -Nity, -Mity, with or without a preceding vowel, expressed by *r*, *l*, *s*, *v*, *nt*, *mt*, respectively.

Arity, Etc.		**Avity, Etc.**	
popularity		depravity	
prosperity		nativity	
majority		brevity	
Ality, Etc.		**Anity, Etc.**	
brutality		urbanity	
utility		trinity	
frivolity		affinity	
Acity, Etc.		**Amity, Etc.**	
tenacity		calamity	
felicity		sublimity	
pomposity		proximity	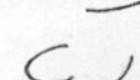

Note: In words ending with *ernity*, the reversed circle is used to express *er* before the suffix sign:

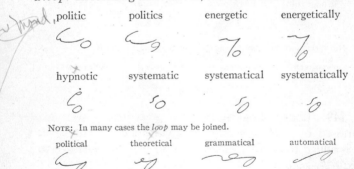

fraternity eternity taciturnity

144. -Stic, with a preceding vowel, expressed by *st.*

elastic domestic artistic atheistic

145. -Tic, with a preceding vowel, expressed by *large circle;* **-Tical,** with a preceding vowel, expressed by a *loop.* In forming derivatives, the other letters are added.

politic politics energetic energetically

hypnotic systematic systematical systematically

Note: In many cases the *loop* may be joined.

political theoretical grammatical automatical

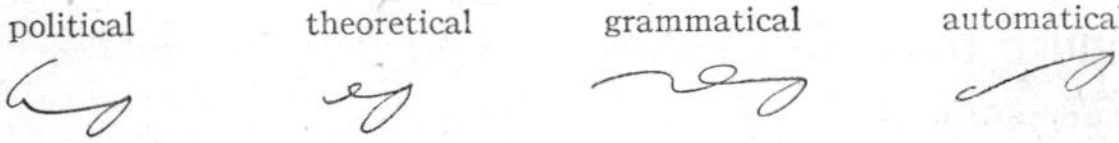

146. -Ntic, with a preceding vowel, expressed by *n.* In forming derivatives, the other letters are added.

gigantic authentic frantic frantically

147. Egraph, Igraph, expressed by *small circle* placed *over* the last character. A *loop* expresses *egraphy, igraphy.* In forming derivatives, the other letters are added.

telegraph calligraph telegraphy telegrapher

148. Ograph, expressed by *o.* In forming derivatives, the other letters are added.

lithograph autograph photograph phonograph

lithography lithographer lithographic typography

NOTE: In most words *ograph* and its derivatives may be joined:

photography stenography stenographer phonographer

149. -Logy, -Logical, with a preceding vowel, expressed by *o* (on its side, as in writing *ol*). The letter *e* is added to express *-logically, s* to express *-logist, n* to express *-logian.*

analogy genealogically geologist pathologist

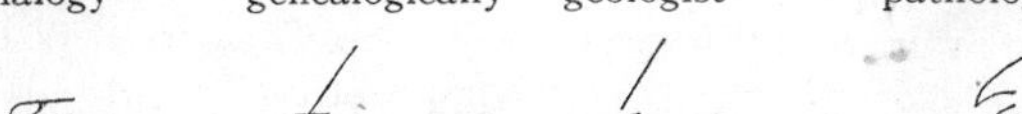

theology theologically theologist theologian

General Exercise

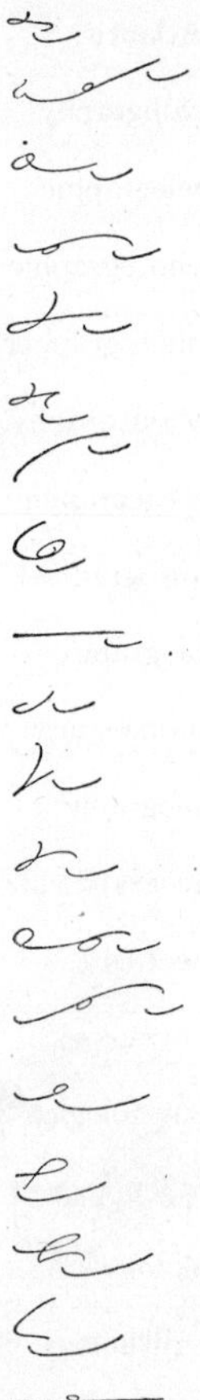

singularity
solidarity
hilarity
regularity
familiarity
sincerity
temerity
priority
minority
authority
futurity
security
alacrity
integrity
reality
nationality
rascality
punctuality
criminality

technicality
vitality
mortality
morality
fidelity
docility
versatility
facility
futility
garrulity
incredulity
capacity
mendacity
veracity
loquacity
complicity
publicity
elasticity
passivity

vicinity
divinity
femininity
humanity
Christianity
extremity
dignity
journalistic
majestic
statistics
automatic
erratic
critic
critical
critically
pneumatic
phonetic
despotic
theoretically
romantic

romantically
Atlantic
calligraphy
telegraphic
photographic
photographer
phonography
stenographic
autographed
biography
mimeograph
geography
geographical
hectograph
physiological
physiologically
psychological
biology
ornithology
chronological

doxology
tautology
analogically
entomology
entomologist
phrenologist
mythology
philology

Reading Exercise

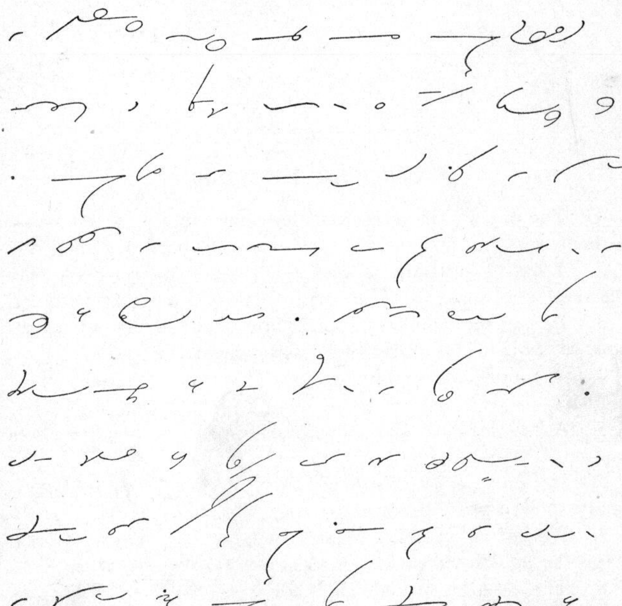

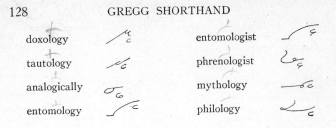

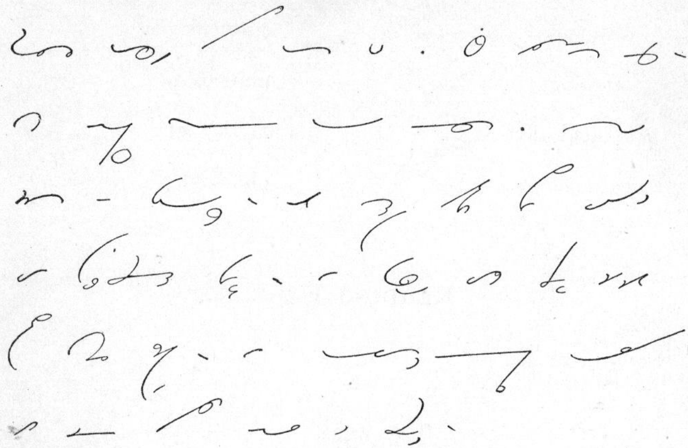

Writing Exercise

1. The importance of punctuality and veracity cannot be overestimated.

2. Tenacity of purpose and fidelity to the interests of the business were qualities which led to his rapid advancement.

3. In making a mimeographed copy of the tabulated report be sure to arrange the statistics in chronological order.

4. The professor of biology sent me an autograph copy of his book.

5. A knowledge of phonetics is an aid to the student of phonography.

6. In the capacity of athletic director the instructor of stenography showed great business ability.

7. We do not question his veracity, but it is necessary for him to go through the formality of filing a bond for security.

8. The stenographer should have a thorough familiarity with the spelling of important geographical names.

NINETEENTH LESSON

ADVANCED PHRASE WRITING

150. Omission of Words. The rules for the omission of words in phrase writing are of great importance, and should be carefully studied. We now give a few more illustrations.

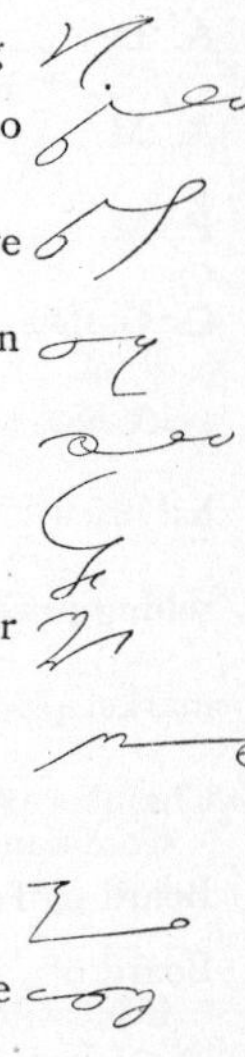

in order to judge	for the time being
in order to prepare	I would like to know
in order to see	I would like to have
on the subject	I am of the opinion
question of time	kindly let us know
sooner or later	bill of particulars
little or no	thanking you for your attention
little or nothing	do you mean to say
in the matter	in such a manner
in the market	on account of the way
on the market	some time or other
up to the time	

151. Intersection. The expedient known as intersection, or the writing of one character through another, is sometimes useful for special phrases. In applying this expedient the writer must rely very largely upon his own judgment. In his daily work as stenographer or reporter, he may find some terms peculiar to the business in which he is engaged occurring so frequently that special forms may be adopted for them which will be brief and yet absolutely distinctive. Very often the intersection of one character through another will meet the exigency. The following are useful examples:

A. D.		Democratic party	
A. M.		Republican party	
P. M.		Progressive party	
C. O. D.		political party	
price list		Baltimore & Ohio (B. & O.)	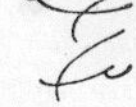
list price		New York Central	
selling price		Michigan Central	
market price		Illinois Central	
Chamber of Commerce		Union Pacific	
Board of Trade		Canadian Pacific	
Board of Education		Northern Pacific	
Board of Managers	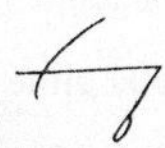	Grand Trunk	

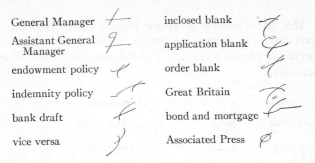

General Manager	inclosed blank
Assistant General Manager	application blank
endowment policy	order blank
indemnity policy	Great Britain
bank draft	bond and mortgage
vice versa	Associated Press

152. Indication of "Ing." *Ing-the*, *ing-that*, *ing-you*, *ing-your*, *ing-his*, *ing-their*, *ing-and*, *ing-this*, *ing-us*, is expressed by writing the word following *ing* in the *ing* position—just as *ington* is expressed by writing *ton* in the *ing* position.

doing the	knowing the
doing his	knowing their
doing your	knowing this
doing their	working and
doing this	having the
giving the	having their
giving their	having your
giving you	coming and
giving us	seeing this
mailing you	wishing that

153. Modification of Word Forms. As previously explained, the forms for certain words are modified to permit of phrase writing. The following are useful illustrations:

Week

past week

last week

this week

next week

for the past week

for last week

for this week

for next week

Few

for a few weeks

for a few months

few weeks ago

few hours ago

Ago

year or two ago

many years ago

Possible

as soon as possible

as near as possible

least possible delay

Early

at as early a date as possible

at your early convenience

at your earliest convenience

at your earliest possible convenience

Sorry

I am sorry to hear

I am sorry to learn

we are sorry to hear

we are sorry to report

we are sorry to say

I am very sorry

you will be sorry

Esteemed

esteemed favor

your esteemed favor

esteemed letter

your esteemed letter

I am in receipt of your esteemed letter

I am in receipt of your esteemed favor

we are in receipt of your esteemed favor

we are in receipt of your esteemed letter

Beg

I beg to acknowledge receipt

I beg to inclose

I beg to thank you

we beg to acknowledge

we beg to acknowledge receipt

Mail

by this mail

by to-day's mail

by this day's mail

by return mail

by mail

by same mail

by early mail

Course

of course

of course it is

as a matter of course

Fact

as a matter of fact

call your attention to the fact

in point of fact

you are aware of the fact

I am aware of the fact

well-known fact

Sure

be sure

to be sure

you may be sure

we are sure

you will be sure

Please

please find inclosed

inclosed please find

please let us hear from you

I would be pleased

we will be pleased

Present

present time

at the present time

at the present moment

on the present occasion

Class

first-class

first-class manner

first-class condition

Again

over and over again

again and again

Account

on account of that

on account of this

on account of my

on account of the fact

Thank

thanking you for

thanking you for your attention

thanking you for your kind attention

thanking you for your favor

thanking you for your letter

I desire to thank you

I have to thank you for

Order

your order

we have your order

thanking you for your order

City

city of Chicago

city of Boston

Department

treasury department
war department
navy department
post-office department
state department
police department
fire department
legal department
inquiry department
credit department
shoe department
furniture department
purchasing department
shipping department
mail order department

Avenue

Washington Avenue
Wabash Avenue
Massachusetts Avenue

Company

and company
railroad company
express company
insurance company
transportation company
telephone company
electric company
electrical company
trust company

Us

to us
write us
please write us
please wire us
kindly give us

Holder

stockholder
shareholder
policyholder

READING EXERCISE

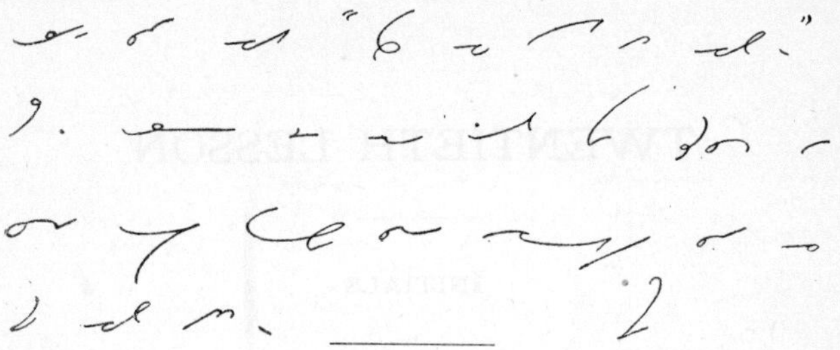

Writing Exercise

1. Gentlemen: As requested we are sending you a copy of our price list giving illustrations and full descriptions of all the articles we now handle. If you are in the market for anything in our line we should like to have our representative call on you with samples.

Thanking you for the inquiry and hoping to be favored with your order, we are

Very truly yours, (66)

2. Dear Sir: A few days ago we received a letter from you in which you asked us to furnish you with information about a firm in this city. We are sorry to report that this firm has never done business with us and that therefore we have no data in our files about it. We have heard again and again that these people are doing a good business and so far as we know their affairs are in first-class condition at the present time. We regret to state that we cannot give you further details.

Yours very truly, (99)

3. Gentlemen: Thank you for the order which has just been received. This order will be filled immediately with the exception of the second item. As our supply of this article is completely exhausted we shall be unable to ship for a few days. We trust that this arrangement will be entirely satisfactory to you and that you will not be inconvenienced by the delay.

Assuring you of our prompt attention at all times, we are

Very respectfully yours, (78)

243

TWENTIETH LESSON

Initials

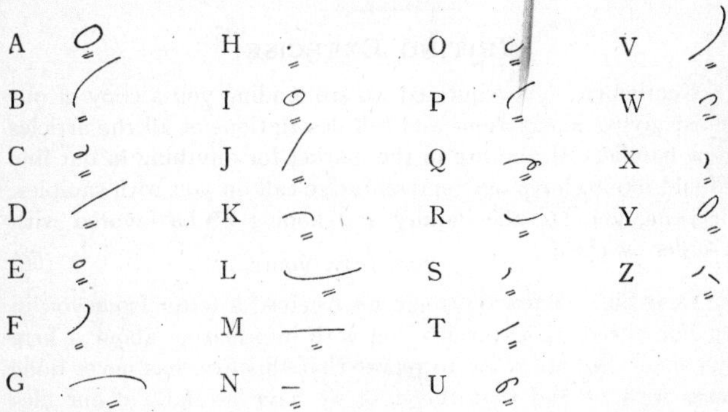

154. It should be borne in mind that there is no context to initials. They should therefore be written with unusual care. Many writers prefer to write initials in longhand, and if this is done a great saving in time may be effected by writing them in small letters and joining the letters, thus:

A. B. Smith C. D. Brown E. F. Jones

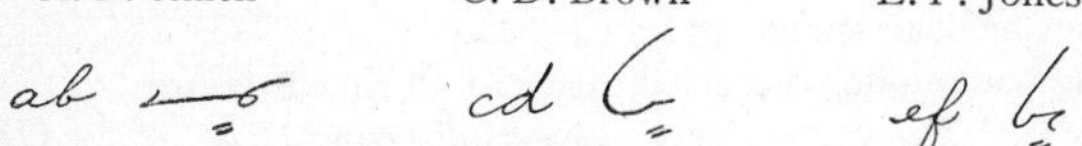

States and Territories

(The contractions used are those adopted by the Post-Office Department.)

Ala.	Ky.	Ohio
Alaska	La.	Okla.
Ariz.	Me.	Oreg.
Ark.	Md.	Pa.
Calif.	Mass.	P. I.
Colo.	Mich.	P. R.
Conn.	Minn.	R. I.
Del.	Miss.	S. C.
D. C.	Mo.	S. Dak.
Fla.	Mont.	Tenn.
Ga.	Nebr.	Tex.
Guam	Nev.	Utah
Hawaii	N. H.	Vt.
Idaho	N. J.	Va.
Ill.	N. Mex.	Wash.
Ind.	N. Y.	W. Va.
Iowa	N. C.	Wis.
Kans.	N. Dak.	Wyo.

Principal Cities

(Arranged in order of population, 1910 census.)

New York	Jersey City	Memphis
Chicago	Kansas City	Scranton
Philadelphia	Seattle	Richmond
St. Louis	Indianapolis	Paterson
Boston	Providence	Omaha
Cleveland	Louisville	Fall River
Baltimore	Rochester	Dayton
Pittsburgh	St. Paul	Grand Rapids
Detroit	Denver	Nashville
Buffalo	Portland	Lowell
San Francisco	Columbus	Cambridge
Milwaukee	Toledo	Spokane
Cincinnati	Atlanta	Bridgeport
Newark	Oakland	Albany
New Orleans	Worcester	Hartford
Washington	Syracuse	Trenton
Los Angeles	New Haven	New Bedford
Minneapolis	Birmingham	San Antonio

155. The terminations *burg*, *ville*, *field*, *port* may generally be expressed by the first letter, joined or disjoined as convenient; and *ford*, by *fd*.

Harrisburg	Evansville	Williamsport
Fitchburg	Knoxville	Oxford
Danville	Springfield	Rockford
Zanesville	Davenport	Hanford
Jacksonville	Newport	Milford

156. A clear distinction should be made between *ton* and *town*.

Johnston	Johnstown	Charleston	Charlestown

157. The names of cities and states may often be joined.

Buffalo, N. Y.	Detroit, Mich.
Rochester, N. Y.	Baltimore, Md.
St. Louis, Mo.	Chicago, Ill.
Minneapolis, Minn.	Denver, Colo.
St. Paul, Minn.	Memphis, Tenn.
Washington, D. C.	Omaha, Nebr.
Boston, Mass.	Louisville, Ky.

158. When the words "State of" precede the name of a state, omit *of* and join the words, if convenient.

State of New York		State of Massachusetts	
State of Nebraska		State of Pennsylvania	
State of Illinois		State of Louisiana	

Points of the Compass, Etc.

159. In certain lines of business the following forms will be found very useful.

north		northeast	
south		southeast	
east		northwestern	
west		southwestern	
northern		northeastern	
southern		southeastern	
eastern		northwest quarter	
western		southwest quarter	
northwest		northeast quarter	
southwest		southeast quarter	

GENERAL RULES

160. When the distinctive appearance of the primitive word-form can be preserved, it is allowable to join to form the derivatives.

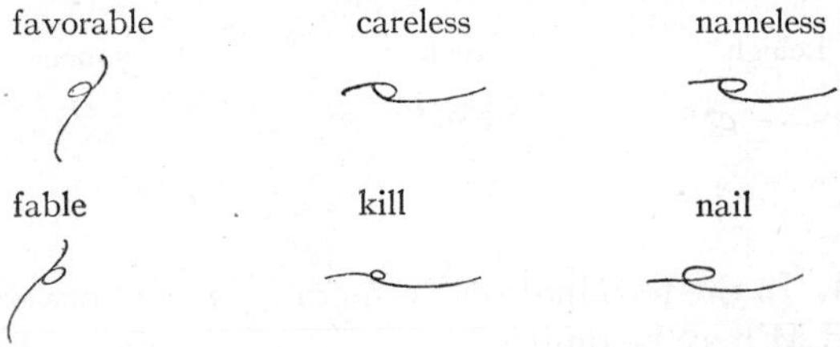

161. If it should be found desirable to indicate with precision the short sound of any vowel, a small curve can be placed beneath the vowel.

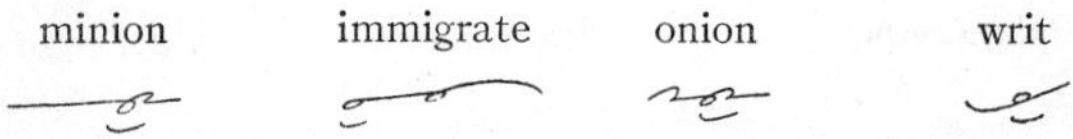

NOTE: This expedient is seldom necessary. It is useful, occasionally, to make a clear distinction between words like *return* and *writ*, *emigrate* and *immigrate*, and between the diphthong ū and ĭu, as in *minion*.

162. The following words are given to illustrate the importance of placing the second circle outside the line when two circles are joined.

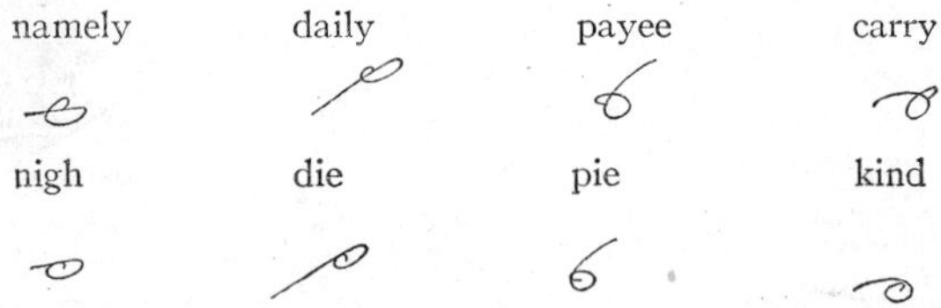

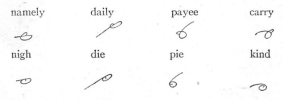

163. There are a few infrequent words, consisting of several vowels in succession — usually Indian names — in which it is more convenient to write the letters separately, and to indicate their connection by drawing a line underneath.

Lehigh ayah yahoo

164. In the termination "n-ment" the jog between the N and M may be omitted.

assignment consignment refinement

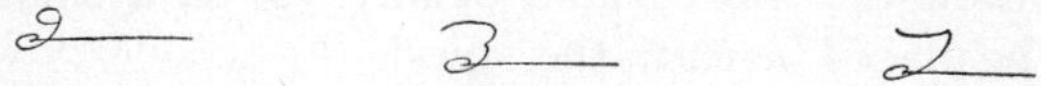

discernment adjournment atonement

165. In the termination *gency*, the N may be omitted.

agency contingency emergency

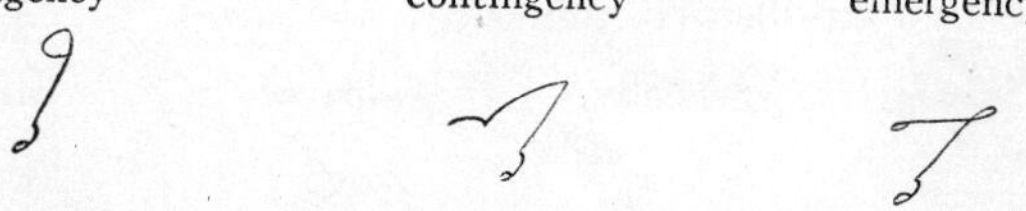

exigency urgency cogency

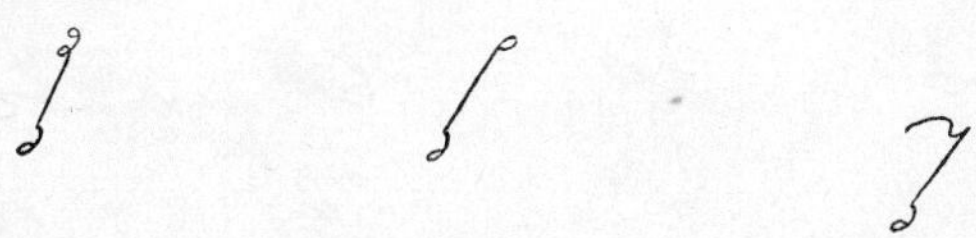

166. A very easy and graceful blend may be secured by joining S to V without an angle in the termination *sive*.

expensive expansive offensive

extensive defensive intensive

167. The Scotch or German *ch*, the Irish *gh*, and the Welsh *ll* may be expressed by a dot over *k*, *g*, and *l*, respectively.

Loch Ach Lough Llan

168. The contracted forms for *hundred* and *thousand* are employed only where these words are preceded by numerals, the article *a* or some such word, as *few*, *many*, *several*. Note the following.

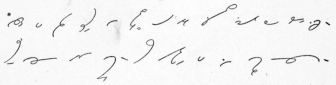

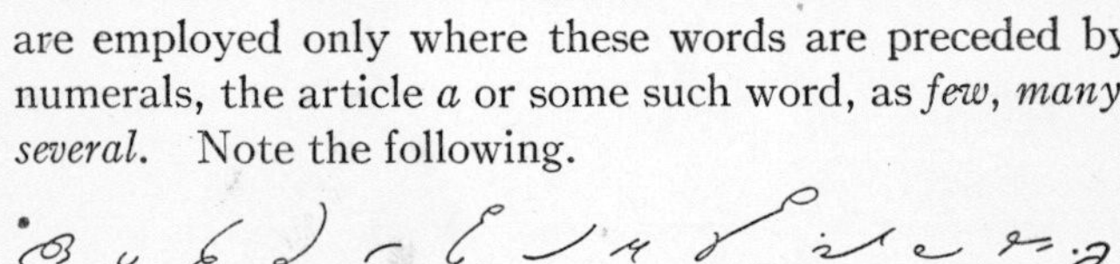

KEY: Thousands of people visited the Exposition and it was said that hundreds were turned away.

Several hundred came to the convention. I have disposed of a thousand copies of the magazine.

Reading Exercise

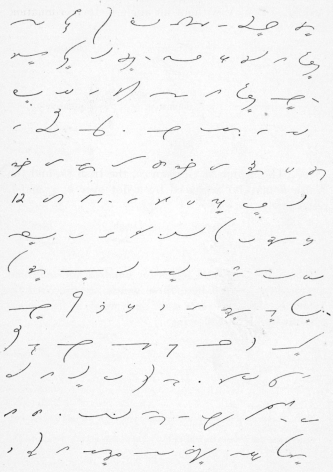

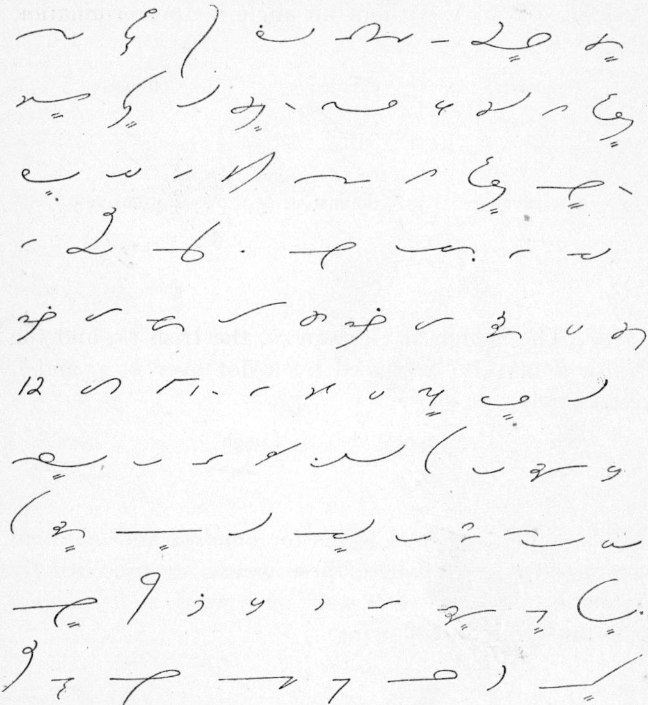

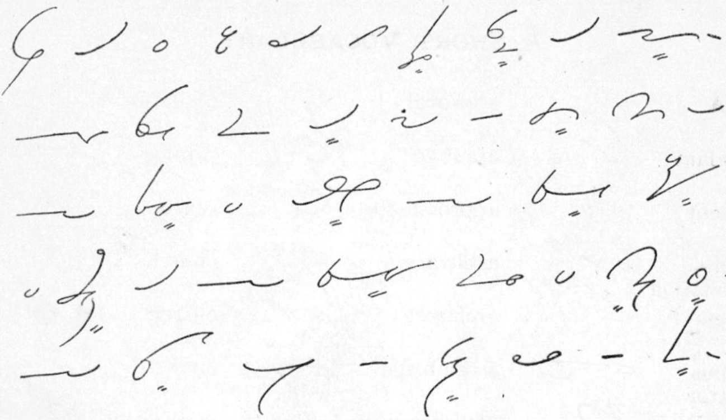

WRITING EXERCISE

1. In the United States, immigration always greatly exceeds emigration.

2. The election writs were correctly made out but the returns were far in excess of all expectations.

3. The laws in the state of New York differ from those in the state of Nebraska in this respect.

4. Almost daily many people are killed through the carelessness of agents of the electric railway companies.

5. The payee of this draft, Mr. J. M. Johnstown, is unknown to us and it will be necessary for him to be identified before we can give him the money.

6. The firm positively declined to accept the consignment of oranges from Florida. They claimed that this shipment had been damaged on account of the carelessness in nailing the boxes as well as by the unfavorable climatic condition during transit.

7. The urgency of the case called for emergency measures and the manager, Mr. R. K. Johnson, after an exhaustive study of the matter decided that the plan proposed by one of the agents, Mr. D. E. Hanford, is the only way out of the difficulty.

A SHORT VOCABULARY

A

abundant
accident
accom-modation
address
adminis-trator
affidavit
amalgamate
amalgama-tion
America
among
amount
annual
another
anxious
appear
appearance
application
apprehend
approval
approve
approximate
arbitrary
architect
assemblage
attach
attorney
authenticity
authorita-tive
automobile

B

bankrupt
behold
benevolent
benignant
boulevard

C

cabinet
casual-ly
catalog
century
church
citizen
civil
civilization
coincide
comparative
conclusive
congregation
consonant
conspicuous
constant
cordial
corroborate
cosmopolitan
count
coupon

to became

covenant
crucible
cultivation
curious

D

danger
dangerous
deceive
default
defendant
degenerate
delegate
delegation
democrat-ic
demoralize
deponent
designate
develop
disadvantage
disaster
discover
dispropor-tionate
dissatisfac-tion
dividend
doctrine
duration

E

earnest
economical
election
engage
English
employer
enormous
envelope
equality
equivalent
etc.
evaporate
execute
executive
exorbitant
expedient

F

flour
fulfill

G

generation
glorious
glory

H

handkerchief
headquarters
hieroglyphic
hitherto
horizontal
husband

I

ignoran-ce / ignoran-t
illustrate

inclosure
incoherent
incomprehensible
indefatigable
indispensable
inherit
instantaneous
instead
institute
institution
intend
introduction
iron

J

jurisdiction
juxtaposition

L

laboratory
legislate
legislation
legislative
legislator
legislature
likewise
litigation
logic
luxury

M

manuscript
messenger
misdemeanor
modern

N

negligence

O

obedient
obligation
o'clock
operation

P

parcel
parliament
partial
passenger
persecute
persevere
plaintiff
practical
practice
precede
prevail
procedure
proceed
production
promulgate
property
prosecute
prospectus
prove

provoke

punctuation

Q

qualify

quarter

R

really

reason

reciprocate

refuse

remunerate

repugnant

resignation

revolution

revolutionize

righteous

rule

real estate

S

salesman

salesmen

secretary

situation

social

specific

specify

steady, study

strengthen

struggle

stupidity

subaltern

support

sympathy

T

testimonial

testimony

thankful

thermometer

thwart

tranquil

U

unavoidable

United States

United States of America

universe

unusual

V

variety

various

verdict

versatile

versus

vocabulary

vocation

volunteer

vote

W

warrant

warehouse

wholesale

withdrew

3/25

SHORTHAND AS A MEANS OF MENTAL CULTURE

(For key, see page 154.)

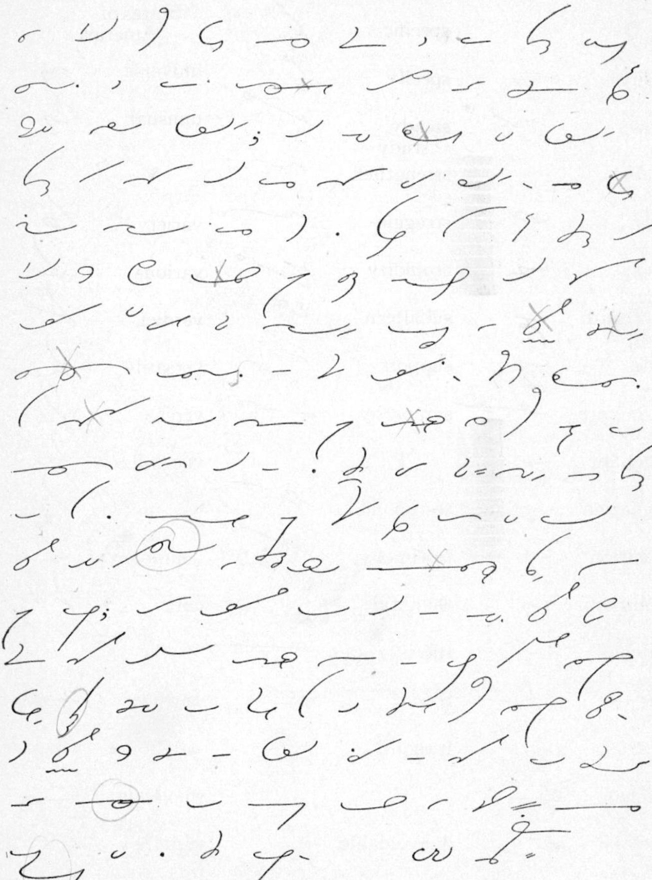

SHORTHAND AS A MEANS OF MENTAL CULTURE

(Key to Shorthand Plate on page 153)

With shorthand every person may form his own books of reference according to his own requirements, and that in the same space as though they were printed; and no selection of printed books would contain and only contain what he wanted. Any person who will collect only for a brief time such facts into shorthand as appear likely to be useful in life, and sometimes read over what is so collected, will find the *ideas* secured again and again recurring in future reading. If this selecting be continued, it will come to be recognized that every newspaper or magazine article, and not a few of the so-called new books, are but a more or less ingeniously contrived patch-work of old ideas, though doubtless the writer in many cases believed them to be original; and the reader will end in knowing *ideas* apart from words, and will recognize them in whatever dress they may be presented, just as we know our friends by their features, however they may be attired. For ideas, as seen in print, heard in words, or felt in the mind, are much like the stars—many reflections of a few originals.—*C. R. Needham.*

SOME GREGG PUBLICATIONS

Prices subject to change without notice

SHORTHAND INSTRUCTION BOOKS

Gregg Shorthand Manual. Revised edition. Bound in cloth.....$1.50

Gregg Speed Studies. Combined textbook and dictation course. A companion for the Manual. 328 pages; cloth............. 1.20

The Gregg Shorthand Junior Manual. A non-vocational presentation of shorthand. 184 pages; cloth.................... 1.50

Supplementary Exercises in Gregg Shorthand. A collection of words, sentences, letters, tests and charts in shorthand and type, arranged in accordance with the division of material in the Manual. 62 pages.................................. .60

Progressive Exercises in Gregg Shorthand. Revised for use with the Manual. Test students' knowledge of each lesson........ .50

Graded Readings in Gregg Shorthand. By Alice M. Hunter. A new reading book adapted to early dictation. 120 pages; cloth .75

La Stenographie Gregg. French adaptation of Gregg Shorthand. By Dr. E. W. Farmer.................................. 1.50

Beginners' Letter Drills. By Alice M. Hunter. Simple business letters written in Gregg Shorthand, supplementing the first six lessons in the Manual. 24 pages; paper.................... .24

Gregg Shorthand Dictionary. New edition, containing the outlines of nearly 17,000 words. Semi-flexible binding.......... 1.50

The New Gregg Shorthand Phrase Book. Contains about 3,000 useful phrases. A great aid in attaining speed............. 1.00

Practical Drills in Shorthand Penmanship. By George S. McClure .16

Taquigrafia Gregg. An adaptation of Gregg Shorthand to Spanish 1.50

German Adaptation of the Gregg Shorthand Manual. By S. V. Greenberg. 91 pages; cloth............................. 1.50

SUPPLEMENTARY

Word and Sentence Drill in Gregg Shorthand. By Mark I. Markett. Contains list of words, sentences, and letters illustrating the principles as set forth in the Manual. All in type. 123 pages; cloth .... .60

Notes on Lessons in Gregg Shorthand. By William Wheatcroft, London. Observations and explanatory notes on the lessons in the Gregg Shorthand Manual. 85 pages; cloth............. .60

Lesson Plans in Gregg Shorthand. By Lulu Westenhaver. 190 pages; cloth ....Net 1.25

Analytical Lessons in Gregg Shorthand. By Mrs. Minnie De Motte Frick. 374 pages; cloth........................... 2.75

Constructive Dictation. By Edward Hall Gardner. Embodies a new idea of teaching practical business English along with dictation. 376 pages; cloth................................ 1.20

FOR THE REPORTER

Shorthand Championship Tests. By Walt H. Mechler. Contains material used in all the shorthand speed contests conducted by the National Shorthand Reporters' Association. 309 pages; cloth $1.20

Gregg Reporting Shortcuts. By John Robert Gregg. A collection of reporting phrases and shortcuts compiled from the work of expert writers. 248 pages; cloth 2.25

The Stenographic Expert (Gregg Edition). By Willard B. Bottome. Adapted to Gregg Shorthand by John Robert Gregg. 263 pages; cloth 2.00

READING BOOKS IN GREGG SHORTHAND

The Sign of the Four. By Sir A. Conan Doyle. 188 pages; cloth .75

Letters from a Self-Made Merchant to His Son. By George Horace Lorimer. Revised edition. 120 pages; cloth .... .75

A Christmas Carol. By Charles Dickens. 56 pages .... .28

The Great Stone Face. By Nathaniel Hawthorne .... .24

The Legend of Sleepy Hollow. By Washington Irving .... .32

Rip Van Winkle. By Washington Irving .... .28

Hamlet. As told by Charles Lamb .... .20

Alice in Wonderland. By Lewis Carroll. 154 pages .... .75

TYPEWRITING

Rational Typewriting. By Rupert P. SoRelle

The New Rational Typewriting (1927 Edition). The latest development in the Rational idea of touch typewriting. 156 pages; cloth 1.20

The New Rational Typewriting (Intensive Course). An intensive course designed for four months' work when two periods a day are devoted to typewriting. 164 pages; cloth 1.20

Typewriting Speed Studies. By Adelaide B. Hakes .... .52

Junior Typewriting. By Elizabeth S. Adams. For Junior High Schools 1.00

Seven Speed Secrets of Expert Typing. By Smith and Wiese. 57 pages; paper .... .60

ENGLISH, SPELLING

Applied Business English and Correspondence. By Hubert A. Hagar and Rupert P. SoRelle. Teacher's key furnished. Text, **$1.00.** Separate Exercises .... .40

Sixty Units in Business English. By Harold S. Brown. A practical course for short term and evening school classes. 162 pages; cloth 1.00

OFFICE TRAINING

Secretarial Studies. By Rupert P. SoRelle and John Robert Gregg. Takes the elementary materials of shorthand, typewriting, English, and the collateral technical subjects and welds them into a smooth working equipment. Adapted to both private and public school courses. 402 pages; cloth. Text 1.40
Laboratory Materials .... .60

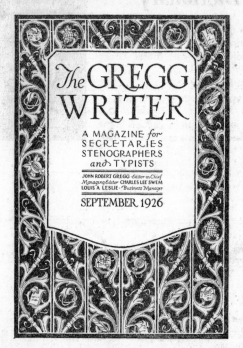